Also by Tony Schwartz

The Responsive Chord

Media: The Second God

TONY SCHWARTZ

Illustrated by Nurit Karlin

ANCHOR BOOKS
ANCHOR PRESS/DOUBLEDAY
GARDEN CITY, NEW YORK
1983

Anchor Books edition, 1983. Published by arrangement with Random House, Inc.

Library of Congress Cataloging in Publication Data

Schwartz, Tony.
    Media: the second god.

    Includes index.
    1. Mass media.   I. Title.
P90.S387   1983   302.2'3
ISBN 0-385-18132-9
Library of Congress Catalog Card Number 81–43920

For Marshall McLuhan

ACKNOWLEDGMENT

I wish to thank Ira Wallach and Jeannette Prussak for their significant contributions to this book.

Contents

Introduction

Tony Schwartz's work in advertising and political communication is legendary: four presidential campaigns; dozens of senatorial and gubernatorial campaigns; television and radio commercials for more than three hundred major corporations. This is complemented by some twenty records, sound for Broadway shows, several award-winning films, and an earlier book on media, *The Responsive Chord*. His impact on the public is both powerful and direct, as he uses media to influence what you buy, whom you vote for, and how you think. For this reason alone, his writings are important. They provide a lucid personal account of how he approaches a communication problem and uses media to achieve an impact. Few people working in media have written about their work in a way that explains the communication principles underlying what they have done. Tony Schwartz explains his methods of work in a straightforward manner that is eminently useful to others who seek to employ media for entertaining, influencing, or stirring up social/political waters.

This book is important as well for those who seek to understand how media function in our society and how all of us are affected by them. Some of these readers may find Tony Schwartz's writings rather frightening, as he describes powerful processes which can be used to create social harm as well as social good. Such concerns are not inappropriate, but they are all the more reason for us to strive to understand the processes through which we are affected by media.

Tony Schwartz brings to this book a fascinating background and approach to work. Aspects of these are helpful to understanding his writings. First, he is not a scholar or researcher by training. He is a craftsman (his craft is communication) who practiced his trade for years and then began to explore the principles underlying his work. In this sense he owes much to John Culkin, Marshall McLuhan, and others who, during the mid to late sixties, prodded him to examine his own work more closely.

In the late forties and early fifties Tony was on the streets of New York recording children's games, street peddlers, and sidewalk musicians. He was not a casual collector but a meticulous archeologist. His early records of street sounds and music are highly edited. The process of editing taught him a great deal about the structure of sounds in everyday life, and the places of rhythm, scale, and social context in giving meaning to sounds. He also studied how children learn to speak (e.g., he has a massive collection of recordings covering his daughter's first three years of life) and how people respond to tones of voice (Robert Frost called this the "Sound of Sense"). This early work with communication in the everyday, non-media world is one cornerstone in his approach to electronic media.

A second important feature of Tony's work is the level of detail. He is a microsurgeon with media. One of his commercials for Coca-Cola involved a solid month of editing sixty seconds of sound. Some consider it his masterpiece. When the commercial is played at half speed (i.e., slowed down), the music, voices, and sound effects are indiscernible, but jumping out at the listener is a complex rhythm which he maintains throughout the commercial whether one is hearing a voice, music, or sound effects. This structural integration at a micro level is difficult to write about, but it is crucial in the process of creating communications. Tony Schwartz's talent, above all, is in creating structural integration from disparate pieces.

A third cornerstone in his work is the utilization of commonplace symbols which have an emotional meaning for nearly everyone. Tony's commercials involve a young girl picking daisies in a field or a mother humming a lullaby to a baby, never a mountain lion sitting atop a used-car sign or anything which a viewer/listener has not likely experienced. Further, his visuals are extraordinarily simple and slow-moving. At times, he has employed one still picture for a 30-second television commercial. If his visuals are simple, they are nonetheless intense. He uses many extreme close-ups, closer than anyone in television. Further, he rarely tries to communicate more than one idea in any commercial.

If one were to try to capsulize Tony Schwartz's approach to commercials, it might be (1) use a single, commonplace symbol which can evoke feelings from your intended audience; (2) attach your product, client, or message to that symbol; and (3) lead the audience *toward* the behavioral effect you desire (e.g., buy the product, vote for the candidate, etc.), but do not tell them what to do explicitly. If you have succeeded in steps 1, 2, and 3, there is a good chance that they will follow through with the behavior you desire.

Regarding Tony Schwartz the person, it is helpful to understand that he is concerned with communication, not politics or business. This has chagrined some who felt he should work on their candidate's campaign free because the candidate was the better man or woman. Others, with less money but intriguing communication problems, have found him endlessly interested. For example, a young student from Yale, Frank Morris, knocked on Tony's door with nine minutes of animated film he had created over a period of five years. No one but Frank Morris himself could understand the film, which purported to be his autobiography. Tony found the film to be a challenging problem and took on the "job." Under the title *Frank Film*, it won an Academy Award the following year, 1973.

Finally, a reader should know that Tony is an extraordinary consumer of the telephone. For one thing, he doesn't like to travel. As a result, he uses the telephone to replace business travel and stay in touch with friends worldwide. He has used these experiences to study how people can employ electronic communication to accomplish what they otherwise do face to face. As he argues in the text, the eighties are likely to be a decade in which the telephone will achieve even greater prominence in our lives, providing many new forms of two-way communication. As these new telephone-based ways of communicating emerge, Tony will undoubtedly be leading the way.

John Carey
New York University

Media: The Second God

The Second God

Ask someone raised in the religious traditions of the Western world to describe God, and this, with idiosyncratic variations, might be the answer:

"God is all-knowing and all-powerful. He is a spirit, not a body, and He exists both outside us and within us. God is always with us, because He is everywhere. We can never fully understand Him, because He works in mysterious ways."

In broad terms, this describes the God of our fathers, but it also describes electronic media, the second god, which man has created.

Radio and television are everywhere and they are always with us. Millions listen to the same networks, hum the same commercial jingles, share with soap-opera characters the testing of souls, the mystery of love and death, the agony of the sinful, and the triumph of the righteous. Stations transmit the same programs worldwide. In cramped apartments in Tokyo, people watch "Charlie's Angels." Lieutenant Columbo tracks down killers in Oslo, Rome, Madrid, and Bucharest. The whole world wanted to know who shot J.R., of "Dallas." And here in the United States we tune in the BBC's "Masterpiece Theatre" or watch Japanese and other foreign films on cable. Two billion people saw a man walk on the moon.

The similarities in people's feelings about God and their attitude about media are evident in the excerpts below. The following statements are taken from interviews I did dealing with religious habits conducted in the early 1960s for the television program "Lamp Unto My Feet":

Woman
I never feel alone, because God is with me.

Child
God is everywhere and I don't know how He could do it.

The following statements are from interviews I conducted in 1967 in the course of researching media habits:

Woman
I never feel alone, because I have my radio and television.
Child
The same programs are in a lot of places.

The media are all-knowing. They supply a community of knowledge and feelings, and a common morality. Many people in the United States, literate and illiterate alike, simply do not read. They receive information from television whether or not they seek that information. It often comes to them in the form of entertainment.

Information is inherent in electronic entertainment, news, and commercials. Media are both a door to the mind and a window on the world. They provide insight and "outsight"—the introduction to hitherto unperceived realities. In one week a single television program, Alex Haley's *Roots,* influenced the way millions of people felt about the life, culture, and experience of American blacks. *Roots* provided the "outsight" about black history, tribal customs, patterns of ritual, all highly exotic to the white viewer who formerly had no knowledge of such things. But *Roots* also provided insight, the sudden understanding that all people share elemental emotions such as love, fear, hope, and despair—the common bonds of humanity that can unite otherwise disparate cultures.

Millions of Americans depend on radio and television, rather than on newspapers, for the news. Their indifference to the print medium has bankrupted newspapers in every major city in the country. In New York City alone we have seen the passing of the *Daily Mirror,* the *World-Telegram,* and the *Herald-Tribune;* only recently the venerable Chicago *Daily News* went under.

The media profoundly affect community attitudes, political structures, and the psychological state of entire countries. God-like, the media can change the course of a war, bring down a president or a king, elevate the lowly, and humiliate the proud, by directing the attention of millions on the same event and in the same manner. Media coverage of the Army-McCarthy hearings, which brought the proceedings into millions of homes at the same moment, ended the senator's career almost instantaneously. Because television coverage of the Vietnam war was so extensive, and because it brought the realities of armed conflict right into America's living rooms, it reduced concepts of heroism, gallantry, and self-sacrifice to the tawdry realities of battle, the suffering, the terror, the desperation, and the agonizing pain, and created a national revulsion against that war. When the American hostages returned home from Iran, the joyful welcome they received was a reflection of how familiar they had become to us through the media, especially television. Televison had brought those people into our homes. We had witnessed their suffering. When we welcomed them back, we felt that we were welcoming friends.

The side effects of media demonstrate the mysterious ways in which they work. These side effects are often more powerful than the intended message. For example, in advertising, whether commercial or political, we typically use media to achieve a straightforward result: to improve the sales of a product or to win votes for a candidate. We can measure these intended results. But the side effects of media campaigns are often elusive, because the people who see and hear these messages do not see and hear them in the same context as the people who devised them. The audience responds to the message in the context of their own lives and problems.

A newspaper whose employees were on strike sponsored a radio message which disclosed the salaries of all the workers, from pressmen to secretaries to office boys. The newspaper's management obviously considered these salaries generous, and the purpose of the message was to evoke certain feelings in listeners: "Well, they're making a pretty good living right now. Why should I miss my paper?"

To a large extent, the message accomplished this primary purpose. But there was a secondary effect that no one could have foreseen. Upon learning the salary levels of these newspaper workers, people flooded the paper's employment office with job applications.

The proprietor of a furniture store advertised over radio for sales personnel who held decorator's certificates. The commercial achieved predictable results and the proprietor found qualified help. Curiously, the help-wanted commercial also increased sales. Potential customers realized that if they patronized the store, trained decorators, rather than mere salespeople, would assist them.

Sometimes the secondary results of a media campaign can take an amusing turn, as in the by now legendary case of a schoolchild who was participating in a spelling bee. When the teacher asked her to spell the word "relief," she spelled "r-o-l-a-i-d-s," taking her cue from the well-known Rolaids commercial.

The media are everywhere and nowhere. They are a spirit, a disembodied entity occupying no space and all space at the same time. The electronic voices we hear have no body. In fact, the entire output of electronic media is invisible. The late Marshall McLuhan called it "angel-like." On television and radio we experience other people, see them and hear them, but they have no corporeal form. The words we hear, the pictures we see on the television screen, exist only in our minds. We make the television picture ourselves as we assemble the scanning dots and from them construct a Walter Cronkite or a Mike Wallace. McLuhan observed, "At the speed of light nobody has a body."

The electronic waves of the media suffuse the atmosphere we live in. McLuhan equated the media environment with the traditional definition of God, whose "center is everywhere and whose margins are nowhere." This relates to the phenomenon of sound. Sound envelops you, because it is spatial, totally environmental. It functions by moving the air. Walk to any part of a room and the sound you hear is substantially the same. To ask, "Where is the center of sound?" is like asking, "Where is the center of the air in this room?" The center is everywhere. Where are the margins of sound? Nowhere. That is what we mean by such expressions as "The room was filled with music." Wherever we sit in a music-filled room, the music is with us. Wherever we are, we are in the center of sound.

The media are within every one of us. The evangelist cries, "Open your hearts and receive God!" We open our eyes and ears and receive electronic media. What we receive exists only in our minds. Just as the idea of God is within us, we retain the memory of the voices and images of the media within us.

We don't need a special house, topped with a steeple, to commune with the second god. He comes into our homes every day and takes his place beside the family.

The second god is accessible to the humble and the mighty, the lettered and the ignorant, the child and the adult. This country has more radios than people, more television sets than bathtubs. The media audience cuts across all class and racial lines. The illiterate share a culture with the literate. The child of the sharecropper and the child of the banker absorb the same information through media.

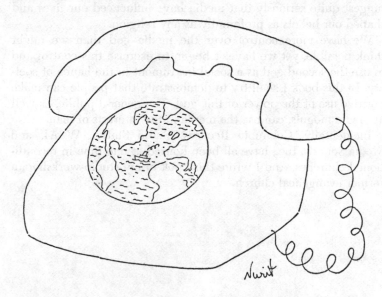

We can talk to virtually anyone anywhere by telephone, and to anyone and everyone everywhere if we have access to radio and television. Any man, woman, or child on earth can hear you as though you were in the same room. We have even heard the man on the moon talk to us in our homes. The second god makes it possible for us to take for granted what was once an exercise of faith: the miracle of speaking and listening to a disembodied voice.

The Judeo-Christian God observes mankind, finds it faulty in many respects, and tries to impose on it a sense of morality, but the relationship between mankind and the second god is different. We, mankind, find the second god faulty in many aspects as we try to impose society's ethics and morality upon the god we made. Many argue that this god is too fond of violence or too engrossed in trivia. At times we may ask this god to change his habits. The second god does not often oblige: although he was created by us, he *appears* to have the power to operate independently.

The analogy between electronic media and God obviously has its limits, and I don't want to carry it too far. However, let me suggest quite seriously that media have influenced our lives and shaped our beliefs as profoundly as any religion.

We have more control over the media god than we might think possible, yet we haven't begun to exercise this control and to use the second god as a social instrument in the hands of society. In this book I shall try to demonstrate that people can make positive use of the power of this god. The general public, as well as media moguls, can use the media in the interests of man.

Incidentally, Columbia Records, Radio Station WBAI, and Media Sounds, Inc., have all been housed at one time in reconditioned churches. And I wrote this book in my studio-workshop, a former evangelical church.

The Post-Literate Society

Nurit

Since the introduction of the telephone, radio, and television, our society has undergone a dramatic qualitative change: We have become a post-literate society. Electronic media, rather than the printed word, and now our major means of non-face-to-face communication.

In pre-literate society, people could transmit information only by word of mouth or by devices such as drums, horns, or smoke signals. In pre-print cultures, almost every member of society worked, and work was everyone's major life experience. People traveled not for pleasure but only when necessity demanded it. The conditions of life severely limited artistic and intellectual horizons. But if knowledge among the masses was sharply limited, it was fairly uniform. Moreover, since children generally participated in work at a very early age and thereby acquired the experiences of adults, there was relatively little difference between the type of knowledge available to an adult and to a child.

With Gutenberg's invention of movable type, print became the major means of non-face-to-face communication, and millions could learn about the world through reading. Literacy naturally became a precondition for anyone who wanted to read books, pamphlets, broadsides, and other printed matter. Education required a level of literacy that millions had not achieved, and literacy required a level of education that millions could not achieve. Print led to a more uneven distribution of knowledge, creating a separation between literate and illiterate, child and adult.

Print dominated communication and structured our society, but this society excluded the child who had not yet learned to read from many aspects of life that adults could read about and understand. Society split into groups related to their reading sources. People read the pamphlets and books approved by their elders or leaders. Catholics did not read Protestant authors. Similarly, political groups had their own newspapers, pamphlets, and essays. There were two levels of censorship: first, from editors and publishers or their equivalent, who shaped the content of books, the thinking of readers, and ultimately the audience; second, from leaders, the mayor, the minister, the head of a family. Both types of censorship had the effect of controlling what information was available to whom.

Although print led to a more uneven distribution of knowledge, it added immeasurably to the amount and variety of knowledge. Print spread information to millions who never before had had access. It made possible the evaluation and comparison of ideas on a vast scale. This encouraged the organized study of science and history, and prepared the way for the Industrial Revolution. The structure of print communication became the structure of a "logical mind" in our society. Because print was the dominant means of communication for so long, we lost sight of its role as a medium and its effect upon thought and knowledge. Print so permeated our environment that we took it for granted as we did the air we breathe. Therefore we were not prepared for the changes that would occur when a new communication medium appeared.

Electronic media signaled a societal change as germinal as the invention of movable type and the printing press. We entered the post-literate age. Growing up in a post-literate environment, our children have received a vast store of information about the world we live in without requiring the ability to read and write, a lack that would have condemned them to utter ignorance in a previous age. Many college educators have remarked that although today's students show low reading and writing levels, they are nonetheless more informed about the world than the literate students of the past. In the words of an article on television and children in *Newsweek* (Feb. 21, 1977), "In general, the children of TV enjoy a more sophisticated knowledge of a far larger world at a much younger age . . . they are also likely to possess richer vocabularies."

Formerly, a city child of two or three who could not yet read had no idea of how a field of wheat sways in the breeze. Today this urban child recognizes the field of wheat from his experience with television. The same preschool child has some understanding of space travel, natural disasters such as tornadoes and floods, and even the terror of war. The midwestern child knows the oceans and tides. The child in Italy knows something of how the child in China lives. The child in Istanbul can recognize the skyline of Manhattan. Little children can identify the voices of national leaders and many other public figures, and they can identify other sounds that television and radio alone have made familiar to them.

This process began with radio and motion pictures. Both of these media communicate without recourse to print. Then television accelerated this expansion of experience and brought billions throughout the world into this new, global system of communication.

Literacy is not a prerequisite for absorbing knowledge from

this world of electronic sound. You don't have to be able to read to talk on the phone, listen to radio, or watch a television program.

Years ago, when literacy was the accomplishment of only a tiny segment of the population, communities supported professional scribes who put down on paper whatever had to be in writing. Today, as writing has reverted to being a special skill, the scribe once more assumes a social function. Many attorneys, for instance, no matter how skilled in the practice of law, do a poor job of brief-writing. They hire brief-writers, "scribes," who have made a specialty of preparing cogent briefs.

Characterizing this as a post-literate society does not mean that print and the written word are dead. Those who speak of the "space age" do not mean that airplanes and automobiles have disappeared, and those who call this the "age of the auto" do not mean that every train has dissolved to dust and all the horses have dropped dead. The post-literate society means simply that the shift in the communication of non-face-to-face information from the written word to the electronic media is now dominant and has a deep and fundamental significance. It is restructuring much of the world. When President Lincoln was assassinated, it took eight months before 85 percent of the people of the United States knew about it. The entire country knew of the assassination of John F. Kennedy in a matter of minutes. Today there is a much greater assumption among people that others share their knowledge. Young people often preface any statement with the expression "You know." This shared information affects the functioning of business, education, government, and all other social areas of life.

Only if we analyze some of the consequences of the shift from a print-dominated communications system to an electronic-media-dominated system can we better solve the economic, social, political, and educational problems of the post-literate age. Such an analysis must begin with an examination of the differences between the print medium and the electronic media.

The Age of Reception

Electronic media are *received* media. Print is a *perceived* medium.

Right at the outset, I'd like to state that I'm using the word "perception" as it was defined in my mother's 1920 dictionary, in which several of the definitions very strongly related to how we *see* the world around us. Although perception can be defined in a much broader and richer manner, I am using the word in this more limited sense in order to really label the difference between media and life that we look out at as opposed to media and life we take in, such as all hearing, and hearing and seeing, from radio, recordings, the telephone, and television. An additional important difference also is the super speed of electronic media.

Spoken language is acquired as a received medium and functions as a received medium. The difference between perceived and received media is critically important. It requires skill and learning for a person to understand most perceived media. Nearly everyone understands received media.

In addition, perceived media require time to be understood. Received media are instantaneous. As a result, people react to received media, whereas they interact with perceived media.

Barring physiological damage or disability, we have no difficulty in seeing or hearing. No one need teach us to see, hear, touch, taste, or smell. However, people do have to be taught to read, and they develop varying degrees of skill in reading. You often hear someone say, "I'm a slow reader." You never hear anyone say, "I'm a slow hearer." If you tell a chatterbox, "You're talking too fast," you are criticizing his style of speech, not your hearing.

On the printed page, you may read a sentence which says, "Her agonized voice was shrill as she screamed, 'Fire!'" Digesting this sentence, the reader comprehends that fire is threatening a frightened woman. It takes a moment, however, to put together (perceive) this information. But imagine being in someone's home when you *hear* the agonized voice of a woman screaming "Fire!" Your reaction to this received message would be immediate.

You might complain that the comparison is unfair. The character in the book is fictional, whereas the person screaming is in a real situation. Then, let us suppose that you are in someone's home and a distraught woman rushes in and hands you a written note that reads, "Fire!" Your first thought might be, Is she crazy? If she's not a mute, why doesn't she yell her head off instead of asking me to read a note? In other words, why is she wasting precious time? Clearly, we respond much more quickly to what we hear than to what we read, even though the difference can sometimes be measured in fractions of a second.

Our brain has stored a great deal of experience with spoken

words. When we hear a word, we react to it at electric speed. This is reception. When we read that word, we go through the mechanics of perception. First we have to construct the word from the letters and then process it intellectually. Even though this can happen quickly, it is still slow compared to hearing and seeing non-print stimuli.

In both print and auditory communication, we can try to attract the attention of an audience by presenting something they can identify with, something that relates to their way of thinking or to their problems. In print, however, a reader must first look at whatever it is we want him to read. If he is in a room and a magazine is lying on a desk, he must get up, reach for the magazine, open it, and flip through the pages before he reads the words the writer wants him to read. The visual and textual manner in which a message is presented must attract him, draw him in. Only then can the writer begin to communicate with him. If the radio or television is on, the person listening or watching does not have to go to the message. The message comes to him. Whatever environment people may be in, all the sound that is in that environment goes into their ears. We can shut our eyes, because we have eyelids. But we cannot shut our ears, because we have no "earlids."

A spoken word never exists in time. It exists only as a series of vibrations. A television picture never exists on the tube. It exists only as a construct of moving light dots. The brain puts together the product of seeing and hearing television, and this process takes place at a phenomenal speed. It is true that a person also assembles in his brain the words that he reads, but those words always stay on the page to be viewed. The difference between the speed of comprehending what we read and reacting to what we see and hear is the difference between the snail's pace and the speed of light and electricity.

At times, we combine reception and perception. We go to a lecture on some abstruse subject such as the crystallography of Mars. We hear (that is, we receive) the information, and as students we take notes. Then we study the notes so that we can perceive later that which we have received. We have also received many other signals not connected with the literal content of what the speaker said. Did he speak loudly enough? Did he make us feel that he was talking to us as individuals? Was he knowledgeable? Was his voice pleasant? Did he remind us of anyone we know?

Traditionally, "communication" means "getting something across," via mail delivery, Western Union, book shipment, newspaper distribution, and the like. It assumes that to communicate you must deliver your message across a gap, transport it from one mind to another. In working with the electronic media I have evolved a "resonance" theory.* The resonance theory of communication is based on the phenomenon of hearing. It concentrates on evoking responses from people by attuning the message to their prior experience. Marshall McLuhan said that "instant information creates involvement in depth." The depth to which he referred is the depth of the mind, and the instant he referred to can be as little as the time difference between reacting to reading and reacting to hearing and seeing.

The transportation theory of communication holds that the content of a communication is that which it contains. Thus a magazine's content is whatever lies between its covers. The resonance theory holds that the real content of an electronic communication is the interaction between the materials on the medium that one receives (the sound of radio or telephone and the combination of sound and image on television) and the stored information in the minds of those who receive the communication. The resonance theory studies the relationship between the message (the stimulus) and the material in the mind of the receiver.

We know that hearing is the brain's reaction to the signals sent by nerves in the ear registering the vibration of sound received through the air. The brain registers a fleeting momentary sound vibration, but it also remembers previous registrations and anticipates future ones. These are the three stages of the hearing process. If I say the word "incompatibility," the sound vibrations of the first syllable, "in," have disappeared by the time you hear the last syllable, "ty." The brain, however, remembers the vibrations that make up the first syllable, and from experience with the language can anticipate the last syllable even be-

---

* See Tony Schwartz, *The Responsive Chord* (Garden City, N.Y.: Anchor Press/Doubleday, 1973).

fore it is pronounced. The words, sentences, sounds, music, that we hear exist only in our brain.

Just as the complete word never exists in time (in the form of sound), the complete television image never exists. A television set does not project an image. It projects a series of dots of light across and down the 525 "lines" on American television sets. These dots are not projected simultaneously. It takes one thirtieth of a second for them to complete two sweeps of the screen, once on each alternate set of lines. You cannot photograph the picture on a television screen if the camera's shutter speed is less than the time it takes for the scanning dots to paint their image completely. A shutter speed of one thirtieth of a second will give you a complete picture. A shutter speed of one fifteen-hundredth of a second will give you only a small fraction of the picture. The total picture never exists.

In viewing television, the brain remembers previous light waves, sees the present ones, and anticipates future ones, putting the "picture" together just as we put words together when we hear speech. This is a startling new development: For the first time in man's history our brains are being used by our eyes and ears in the same manner. In other words, with electronic media we now "see" by the same process by which we have always heard.

When the printed word is the primary medium for the dissemination of knowledge, a teacher gives students reading assignments. Later the teacher will test the students to see how much they remember of what they have read. The purpose of such a test is to measure what they could recall, or what they have "learned." But when we communicate with electronic media, learned recall is not as relevant as evoked recall. Evoked recall functions with electric speed. For instance, if someone says to you, "For the rest of your ——," you will have filled in the word "life" before he gets to say it. (In reading we would also assume the word "life," but we would arrive at it through thinking, rather than reacting.) This is the area of expectation. Meaning is the contextual relation of what we hear to our previous experience. Recorded or previous experience is an important part of the hearing and understanding process.

Since the attitudes and beliefs that people bring to an electronic communication determine what they take from it, the skillful electronic communicator should be aware of what is inside the minds of the people he wants to reach, so that he can find a link between his material and those who receive it. Research aimed at uncovering this will tell how to evoke a response that will move people most effectively, based on a correct assessment of their stored attitudes and experience.

Commercials I used in Patrick Moynihan's senatorial campaign illustrate this process. During that campaign (and after), New York City was in deep financial trouble. New Yorkers wanted a senator who they felt would fight in Washington for the survival of their city. Our research revealed how the voters assessed the senatorial candidates. According to this research, people considered Patrick Moynihan to be a strong and forthright fighter. These feelings derived from the public's knowledge of his performance when he was the U.S. ambassador to the United Nations, knowledge gained from both press and television reports. This indicated to me that political commercials for Moynihan should evoke the memory of his fighting performance in the United Nations. This evoked feeling could then be transferred to suggest that he would bring his fighting spirit to Washington in defense of New York City. When Moynihan himself said on those commercials, "When I'm in Washington you'll know I'm there," people believed him. It wasn't just an empty campaign promise, because people remembered that when Moynihan was in the U.N. they really *did* know he was there. The commercials simply transferred an existing feeling into a new context.

Another example can be drawn from a radio commercial for Bamberger's Department Store, in New Jersey. The radio commercial began with the line "Bamberger's is having a special sale of the most comfortable mattresses you can think of." To arrive at this line I used "presearch," a term I apply to research conducted before the creation of a commercial. Presearch helps determine the character of a commercial. Presearch told why this ad would be effective for Sealy mattresses but for none other. Ten people had been asked what came to their minds when they heard the words "comfortable mattresses." Nine of them responded "Sealy." Since the sale featured Sealy mattresses, the commercial, which mentioned the name "Sealy" only near the end, evoked the proper response.

For over five centuries our basic means of non-face-to-face communication was the printed word. As a consequence, the study of learning and the study of communication have dealt primarily with how we see, understand, and make use of the information we obtain primarily through reading. But in a world in which we are so extensively involved with non-print communication—radio, telephone, and television—we need to set up a separate study of reception, because electronic media do affect us much differently from the way the world of print did. Schools have not yet offered such programs, and yet they are vital if we are to understand and control the vast changes that will come about in business, communication, education, statesmanship, and every other area of life, because of the electronic media.

In this chapter I have used only commercials to illustrate the concept of reception, although it applies to many other areas of electronic communication. In the chapters that follow, I will go into other dimensions and ramifications of reception.

Replay:
The Recall of
Experience

Cognition is the act of knowing or perceiving. Recognition (re-cognition) involves perceiving again that which we already know. Until recently, the cognition of an experience always had to precede recognition. For example, if I recognize someone on the street, I obviously know him from some previous experience.

The speed with which we receive information through the electronic media sometimes reverses the sequence of cognition and recognition. In certain circumstances things happen so fast that we "recognize" the event through previous experience and then find out what actually happened with the help of an audio or videotape or video disc. If you watch sports on television, you have undoubtedly seen someone score a touchdown without knowing exactly how it was done until you saw the replay. You observed the effects of what happened (the touchdown) at nor-mal speed, and this was recognition. But you saw what really happened and how it happened (cognition) only during a replay at slower speed.

Replay is more than a toy, a trick we perform with a piece of tape. Instant replay is, in fact, one of the more important developments in human history.

In pre-literate societies, tale telling was the earliest form of replay. But tale telling was slow and subject to distortion, since whoever repeated the tale was apt to embellish it or forget significant incidents. Then came the epic poem, the liturgy, the lay of the minstrel, and the ballad, all of which acted as mnemonic devices. Rhythm or rhyme in a poem or ballad helped ensure accuracy in subsequent retellings. "Columbus sailed the ocean *blue* in fourteen hundred and ninety . . . seven"?

The printed word makes accurate replay possible for anyone who can read. Rereading (that is, replaying) a series of words on a page, we can go over the same thought or message as many times as we please, savor passages that engage us, ponder over a complicated idea, or discover in the words nuances that we missed on first reading. The ability to replay the printed word made possible great leaps forward in science and history.

We are largely unaware to what extent replay has enriched our lives. Don't think of replay only as television repeating a shot of a third baseman miraculously spearing a line drive. All records, photographs, movies, and videotapes are replay. We see most of the news on television in the form of replay. The retail clerk who takes your credit card uses a form of instant replay in checking your personal credit standing through a telephone data bank.

Product, corporate, and political advertising; academic and business education; and such fields as medicine, law, science, and government have only begun to appreciate the importance of instant replay by electronic media and the control it gives over the interplay of cognition and recognition. Using a computer, your doctor can now play back your medical history in a few seconds and determine all the details of your health patterns for as long as he has attended you. In those few seconds, a businessman can see spread out before him the buying patterns of an important customer. Instead of painstakingly searching libraries, lawyers can retrieve a century of legal precedents at the push of a few buttons.

I based one political campaign almost exclusively on replay. I was working for a senatorial candidate who was challenging an incumbent of fourteen years. The commercials in our campaign simply replayed in rapid succession the incumbent's statements, made over a long period, to show the inconsistencies in his position. The quick replay revealed a pattern that was not visible in the real-time experience of the incumbent's fourteen years in office.

For the New York *Daily News* I designed a 30-second television commercial that replayed all the headlines of the previous month. We produced this commercial one hour after the last paper of the month came out, and it was ready to run the next day. When the audience saw this replay of headlines from the month just ended, they felt that they were seeing all the news and history of that month that had been brought to them sharply, directly, and quickly in the *Daily News*. Here were the headlines of August 1976 as they appeared on television on the first day of September:

> HURLS LYE, HITS 23 COPS IN SIEGE
> 63 DIE IN COLO. FLASH FLOOD
> MYSTERY FEVER KILLS 16 IN PA.
> 20 DEAD, 115 ILL IN PA. MYSTERY
> 18,000 STRIKE AT 16 HOSPITALS
> LEGION FEVER RAPIDLY EASING
> HOSPITALS FEAR NEW WALKOUTS
> CITY HOSPITAL STRIKE ENDS
> CASTRO PLOTTER IS FOUND SLAIN
> BELLE SLAMS ACROSS LONG ISLAND
> PANEL CUTS OFF-DUTY TIME
> 4 DIE IN EL AL HIJACK ATTEMPT
> PRESS BUCKLEY TO DROP HIS BID
> FORD BEATS GUN ON 2 GOP PLANKS
> FORD, REAGAN DUEL ON RULES
> FORD WINS KEY VEEP TEST
> VOTE SWITCHES PUT FORD AT TOP
> FORD WINS TEST, ALMOST HAS IT!
> FORD WINS IT!

FORD TO CARTER: LET'S DEBATE
REAGAN: UNITY IS UP TO FORD
AIDE RATES CARTER DEBATE UNDERDOG
CARTER DEFINES FOREIGN POLICY
ATTICA INMATES GO ON STRIKE
PHONY OVERTIME COSTS CITY $1M
CITY CRIME HITS ALL-TIME HIGH
INMATE STRIKE EASES AT ATTICA
I WANT TO WIN NEW YORK: FORD
39 DIE IN TWO AF JET CRASHES
FORD ASKS $1.5B FOR U.S. PARKS
HOW DOCS CHEAT ON MEDICAID

Each full front page of the paper was on the screen for approximately one second. An electronic beep accompanied each change of headline. In the first few seconds of the commercial the announcer said, "Did you see what happened in August?" At the end of the commercial, he said, "See what happens in September every day in the *Daily News*."

Electronic replay can be far more effective than the printed word in preventing the distortion of history. The written word is a writer's impression of an event, and one writer's impression can be notoriously different from another's. I once edited tapes of a series of congressional hearings and I discovered that the written transcripts of those hearings differed markedly in many places from recordings of the same hearings taken off the air; too often people see and hear whatever fits their preconceptions. In some situations, of course, electronic replay can be used to distort history, and only vigilance can prevent this.

Playback (and speed changes during playback) have great value when we deal with complex movement. A film made by a group doing aerodynamic research illustrates this. The group was studying the landing patterns of different varieties of birds. One sequence in the film showed large sea birds in the act of landing on a beach. A slow-motion replay revealed things that the unaided eye could not catch, such as the positioning of the wings and legs, and the extension of certain feathers.

In the same way that a high-speed sequence of stills enables us to see motion, high-speed replay enhances our ability to recognize community, national, global, and astronomical patterns.

On the weather segments of television news programs, meteo-rologists often replay a series of satellite photographs shown in rapid succession, revealing the large-scale movements of weather fronts, storms, hurricanes, and other natural phenomena.

Today we have replay capacity in print, print visual, pictures in motion, and sound. Replay, and the ability to vary its speed, has shown us how flowers grow and horses run, how molecules move and insects reproduce. The various combinations of com-puter, videotape, microfilm, and other forms of visual and audi-tory recording equip us to replay many important events in the historical and cultural development of man. A hundred years from now our descendants will be able to replay the Watergate Hearings, and by both seeing and listening to the participants, examine subtleties, attitudes, and manifestations of personal feel-ing that no print account could fully convey. We ourselves have seen the Bert Lance "deconfirmation" hearings, Knapp Commis-sion sessions, and other public replays of events that previously took place in relative secrecy.

Musicologists have written countless books speculating on the manner in which Johann Sebastian Bach played his music, the tempos he employed, how he executed his embellishments. But imagine what it would mean to the world of music today if we could replay, in sight and sound, the music of Bach as per-formed by the master himself.

Today we have new media whose replay offers us a dramatic potential to achieve new dimensions in study, meaning, and con-tent. One is the computer, but at present its use is confined pri-marily to the area of print-related material. The computer is just beginning to move into the graphic area, and eventually it will operate in the area of sound. With the computer we can in-stantly trigger back stored auditory and visual material.

Another medium, one that is available to the average man and woman, is the video disc and the half-inch videotape re-corder. Using the video laser disc, we can play back any frame of prerecorded material and any sequence of frames, and we can also play it back in motion. We can slow the motion or speed it up. The new videotape recorders are not only valuable as a source of stored entertainment but also as a new tool in study and research. Some of these machines can be programmed to record any sequence of events up to five hours' duration over a two-week period. Recording at the slower speed results in fair quality, while recording at the faster speed results in good quality. This means that a three-hour tape can record three hours of good quality or four and a half hours of fair quality. Such a machine can record any segment of any program. It can, for instance, record seven, eight, or ten minutes of a program, and it can be made to switch automatically from station to station. If the owner of such a machine also has a video camera, he can record live visual material.

What does it mean when a machine can record sound and picture at normal speed, and during replay, stop at any given frame, advance frame by frame, and play forward or backward? It means that we have a new tool for the study and careful observation of visual material. This form of playback opens a new world in which we will be able to play back history, record sequences of events, develop pattern recognition at high speeds. Such a machine can help in teaching medical and surgical techniques. Music students can use it to study famous violinists and pianists and observe their fingering. Instant playback can quickly determine the soundness of any disputed call in athletic contests. Motion is now easily studied. Such machines can also help to analyze the problems of politicians as public speakers, observe patients' emotional problems, and assist the study of historic events by juxtaposing them to observe their relation to each other.

McLuhan said that scientists of the past organized knowledge for convenience of retrieval, but he found that for himself discovery came from organizing things that he did not know, and then studying them. These machines can serve that function: the organization of material which we do not yet understand.

The Essence of
the New

Man habitually treats the new as an extension of the old and fills new media with the old media as their content.

We have always found that our thinking is related to the structure of our communications. In pre-print, auditory cultures, only the present existed, and the old was considered an extension of the new. Between the pre-print and the electronic culture lay many centuries of print-dominated culture. On a printed page, each line is an extension of the previous line, and in a sentence, each word extends from the previous word. The printed word fostered the concept that the new is an extension of the old.

We often say that the present makes no sense without an understanding of the past, but in every area of life and work the opposite may be equally true. When the introduction of the automobile revolutionized transportation, people dubbed it the "horseless carriage," investing the new with the old as its content.

It takes time before those who work with what is new stop treating it as an extension of the old. The first time I ever went out to work on sound for a television commercial, I had to prepare a track for film. I went to a reputable sound studio. I mixed the track and thought it was excellent. Then I brought it back to my workshop and played it on a quality recorder. The track sounded terrible.

Convinced that something was wrong with the studio's equipment, I went back to complain. They played it for me again and it sounded fine. Then I realized that they had mixed the sound in a large room with large speakers and a long projection distance. They were "equalizing" the sound track to accommodate theater acoustics. Their recording room was in reality the size of a theater. My workshop where I listened was actually a converted living room, and it sounded different there.

The people in the sound studio had first learned about equalizing sound in order to fit the needs of film and the acoustics of the movie theater, and they had simply transferred those methods to the television medium. Moreover, they insisted that film itself had certain limitations which made it difficult for them to give me what I wanted.

I fought this idea. I tested the capability of film and found that it could take the full spectrum of sound. I finally got what I wanted: a sound track designed for radio or television and the acoustics of the home.

My father was a civil engineer who built many radio-station studios. I remember his showing me how a radio studio was hung internally within another room. The goal of studio design was silence. I soon learned that recording studios are not the best place to make recordings. They are better as places to bring your recordings for editing when you want total silence in order to hear what you have recorded.

Since early recording equipment was all but immovable, it was housed in a permanent location, a studio that had to be designed for silence to keep out any sound that might accidentally disturb the recording. Yet those quiet sound studios were not really good places to record, in part because the "perfect acoustical situation" has no real relation to life. When portable equipment was developed, in the 1940s, sound studios became obsolete. It was not necessary to bring the band to the studio, once we could bring the recording equipment to the band. We no longer needed the studio to re-create what was created elsewhere.

This does not hold true for today's electronic music, which employs many sound tracks and overlays. The studio may be the only place where such music can be recorded. For this reason the Beatles' song "A Day in the Life" could take shape only in a studio. The Beatles could never perform it live at a concert, because it was made of various components that were done at different times. It is said that the Beatles turned down an offer of one million dollars to perform it on "The Ed Sullivan Show" for this reason. Recently a group offering a concert-style entertainment called *Beatlemania* has been performing "A Day in the Life," but they can do it only because they use prerecorded material as part of their performance.

Today we can record wherever the environment is consonant with what we are doing. We do not need absolute silence, because sound itself is not noise. Noise is unwanted sound, and it is quite possible to find places to record where the surrounding sound is not unwanted. If you want to record an office worker in an office, the sound of typing is appropriate. If you record a woman in a kitchen, the whistle of a kettle or the sound of food frying may not be unwanted.

In the infancy of motion pictures, producers took books and plays and attempted to transfer them to the new medium. The film studio was nothing more than a theater stage picked up from Broadway and dropped down in Hollywood. Movie theaters covered the screen with a theater curtain. Before the picture began, the curtain rose as though to reveal a stage set. In the old silent movies, artists even drew theater curtains on the sides of every frame of printed dialogue.

The unwieldy proportions and technical limitations of the early motion-picture camera did not give producers enough mobility to break away from the trap of planning what happened in front of cameras. The planning took the form of scripts.

Then film makers began to discover the special qualities of the medium. Film editing became a unique art. Film editing consists of deciding what footage to eliminate, which angles are better, when and where to cut from one scene to another, whether the camera should focus on someone who is speaking or on someone who is reacting to the speaker, and similar matters. Film editing was the basic technique which freed the motion picture from the restrictions of the stage. In live theater, everyone in the audience has a fixed seat, and what he sees on the stage depends on where he is sitting. In a movie theater, everyone sees exactly the same thing on the screen. Everyone has the same "seat."

Film equipment became more sophisticated. The electronics industry developed portable magnetic recorders. Film makers could now go out and film "life." The walls of the studio came tumbling down. The world was both studio and stage, the camera an instrument for recording life as it happened; the real-life material could be edited into "real-life" drama.

Early phonograph recordings illustrate how the new is first used as an extension of the old. These early recordings offered us only a repeat of what concert artists had previously performed before a live audience. In Edison's "perfect" studio the brass horn through which sound passed to the cutting tool on the recording device was 128 feet long. Because of the size of the equipment, any musical artist who wanted to record had to go to the studio. Today's quality recorder weighs under twenty pounds and sometimes as little as five pounds, and it can be battery-operated.

Early radio was fully scripted, thereby making the spoken word exclusively the read word. When we listened to early radio we were actually listening to print.

In addition to being a medium for transporting the "printed" word, radio also relied on another old form of communication: public speaking. Public speaking was considered to be an art, while private speaking was not acceptable on radio. The stations and networks employed men and women who had what were called "radio" voices, sonorous, dignified, stilted—voices suited to the podium, not the living room. Such voices helped overcome the poor reproduction quality of early radio, and no radio announcer or performer ever dreamed of departing from a script. To ad lib, or interpolate, was considered highly unprofessional, something akin to an actor's suddenly inserting his own soliloquy during a performance of *Hamlet*.

Standards of professionalism were unrealistically rigid. In 1937, Herb Morrison, a Chicago news announcer, went to Lakehurst, New Jersey, to cover the arrival of the dirigible *Hindenburg* after its maiden trans-Atlantic flight. Morrison began his broadcast calmly and objectively, but when the *Hindenburg* burst into flame and he saw passengers fall screaming to their deaths, he broke into sobs. This was considered unprofessional, and Morrison lost his job. Years later, while covering the Kennedy assassination, Walter Cronkite also broke into sobs. Far from considering him unprofessional, most viewers looked upon the incident as a tribute to Cronkite's humanity. No one dared criticize his conduct or accuse him of failing to maintain the proper professional objectivity.

In the years between the *Hindenburg* disaster and the assassination of Kennedy, radio hosts such as Arthur Godfrey and Henry Morgan introduced a more relaxed and personal, conversational style, uncorseted by the restrictions of script and attuned to the intimate character of the medium itself. They talked as though they were addressing an audience of one, rather than an audience of millions, and in so doing, made "private speaking" an art in its own right by developing the correct verbal projection distance for radio in the home.

Radio was shackled to print until the 1950s and 1960s, when improvisation and informal discussion helped it realize its own character. Radio, once "read," is now "said."

When radio and television came along, advertisers at first treated them as an extension of the old. They read from their printed ads. They used their old, print-oriented research methods to guide them in evaluating commercials. Since print deals with perception, research for print advertising always tried to determine what people remembered about or learned from an ad they had read. But to rely on research that determines what an audience remembers or learns after hearing a commercial is of little help when dealing with the new, received media. What matters is how people are affected by what they see and hear, and how a commercial connects with their feelings and concerns.

Television began by imitating the motion picture. A series of videotapes I made of the famous gospel singer Mahalia Jackson illustrates this. The tapes show Mahalia Jackson as she appeared on early film, later film, early television, later television, and modern television. Early television presented her as if she were in a 1940 movie. She appeared on a 14-inch screen as a full figure some six to seven inches tall, inconsequential, Lilliputian, in no way able to reach visually or emotionally into a living room. It was as though a small statuette were singing. Yet, presented in a movie theater with a large screen, Mahalia Jackson would have appeared as an imposing figure able to communicate effectively with a theater audience on a one-to-one basis.

The methods of presenting Mahalia Jackson went through various transformations as she was presented on different media. During the most recent program, televised a short time before her death, the screen was entirely filled with her head, and the projection of her voice was also more intimate. In a theater, a singer with no electronic devices must sing out to reach all paying customers, including those in the rear of the second balcony. But when we listen to radio or television, the distance the voice must travel is basically from the singer's mouth to the microphone, a matter of a few feet or even inches, and then from the home loudspeaker to the listener's ear, another few feet at most. The distance from the transmitter to the home has no meaning, since the transmitted signals are not sound waves. They are converted into sound waves only after they enter the television or radio set.

Writers who have worked in the electronic media have found that their function has changed radically. Before the advent of these media, the writer had perhaps the most important role in communication. Now writing is only one of many component parts. As in any endeavor, the thinking behind the process of electronic communication is most important, and the director, the producer, and many technicians can participate in that thinking. Materials can be recorded, edited, and designed with audio and videotapes. Writing still plays a role in electronic communication, but material for radio and television can now be produced without a writer.

Ironically, many authors nowadays don't "write." They can produce a book simply by talking into a tape machine or recording the words of others, and then hiring someone to transcribe and edit. Newspaper reporters rely as much on recording devices as on pads and pencils.

Composers, too, now often do without a written musical score, the counterpart of the written script. Many musical groups do their composing, arranging, and editing solely on tape.

The urge to see the new as an extension of the old has shown up in the business practices of many electronics companies which have bought up magazine and book publishers. The parent companies try to utilize the sales staffs that come with their acquisitions. After all, if publishing companies know how to sell books to schools, why can't their sales staffs sell cassettes and videotapes to the same schools? Won't a book company give an electronics company a built-in sales staff for the educational market?

It doesn't work that way. The products are very different. The man who knows how to sell books may end up trying to sell cassettes to the wrong people. The best place for audio or videotapes may not be the library. After all, most libraries have the equivalent of a large sign that says "Shhh!" A videotape's value is its difference from a book, not its similarity to a book.

When looking for someone to fill a job vacancy, most people advertise in the "Help Wanted" columns of a newspaper. On many occasions I have used radio to advertise job openings, and in every case radio gave us much better results than newspaper ads. The reasons are simple. Only those people who are looking for work read the "Help Wanted" ads, but radio reaches everyone listening, the employed and the unemployed alike, and if what you are offering in the way of work is very attractive, you may get responses from skilled people who are employed but who consider your offer an improvement over what they have. I have done such "Help Wanted" ads on radio for Bamberger's and Data General, and I have also used radio to advertise for students for the University of Illinois. (In the case of a university advertising for students, a newspaper ad reaches only those people who read the educational section, whereas radio reaches a more general audience, some of whom may be inspired to think about going back to school.)

Each electronic medium came into its own only when we recognized its newness and stopped trying to use it as a container of the old.

Rearranging
Space and Time

"I don't know who discovered water," says a friend of mine, "but it certainly wasn't a fish."

We pay little attention to an environment until our relationship to that environment or the environment itself changes. Ask people what they will need to survive in the coming year. You will get many answers but very few will mention air. Air is an environment that totally surrounds us and therefore goes unnoticed.

In communications we tend to become aware of the basic characteristics of a medium only after a new one has replaced it or coexists with it.

When electronic communication developed in the late-nineteenth and the early-twentieth centuries, we were able to observe to what extent print had dominated Western civilization. The telephone, telegraph, and wireless made us much more aware of the print environment and its impact on us, because we now had a choice of media when we wished to communicate. Before we make choices, we make comparisons.

We are best able to evaluate an environment when we can leave it, step outside it. When we move to a new apartment, we have a fresh appreciation of the size and convenience of the old one, or else we wonder how we ever could have lived in such cramped quarters.

Years ago it never entered our heads that the air in our community was polluted. This judgment came when we were able to "leave" that air and make a quick comparison test. We "left" that air when we installed air-conditioning and when we traveled by plane. Stepping out of the filtered air in our air-conditioned room, we noticed the difference between that air and the air we breathed outside. On plane flights we could look down and observe the murkiness of the city air far beneath us. Before air-conditioning and air travel, people simply said, "It's nicer in the country" or "There's a lot of industrial haze in Pittsburgh," without directly associating haze with pollution.

When standing close to his canvas as he paints, an artist is involved, but when he steps back to see what he has done, he is more detached. Distance provides a different perspective.

Before the advent of electricity, the speed of all communication other than person-to-person conversation depended on two factors: time and distance. How long did it take a letter to reach England by ship in 1850? How many men had to ride horses over how many miles and for how many hours to bring a letter from Boston to the Continental Congress in Philadelphia? Today, with microphones, we can talk instantly to anyone anywhere.

Before electricity, a person's farthest range of vision was from the vantage point of a crow's nest on a ship or atop a lofty peak. Today our range of vision is limitless. Television is the telescope or window through which we can look at every corner of the earth. Sitting in our homes, we can watch the coronation of kings, death on the battlefield, flood and fire—wherever they are taking place. We can see through walls, across oceans and mountain ranges, and even examine the landscape of planets and moons.

Nurit

Man's hearing and sight evolved over thousands and thousands of years. Basic changes in the structure of the human body were hardly perceptible. Then technology surpassed evolution and in seconds gave new dimensions to man's eyesight and to his hearing.

In pioneer days, people who set out for the West in their Conestoga wagons left behind them a world with which they could no longer communicate. True, there was mail service of a sort, but it was notoriously unreliable. The pioneer who left friends and relatives behind might never talk to them or see them again. Today we have that vital link of direct communication with those we love no matter how distant they may be. The parent can talk to the child away at school. One spouse can speak to the other who is on an overseas business trip. The traveler is lonesome no more. On the road he has the company of his car radio, and if he is a CB-er he can have two-way communication.

The speed of sound is no longer only 1,100 feet per second, or 728 miles per hour. It is also 186,000 miles per second. Electricity and its speed have all but eliminated distance and time as factors in communication. To understand this, it is useful to retrace the development of audio recording.

The genesis of the invention of the phonograph lay in Edison's efforts to increase the output of the Atlantic cable. His concept was to record the Morse code's dots and dashes, play them back at faster speed, and thus increase the number of words transmitted per minute through the cable. He did not foresee, however, exactly how his device would become the grandparent of other information-storing machines: the phonograph and the computer.

Edison had remarkable foresight, but some of the uses he predicted for the phonograph never materialized. It remained for tape recording to fulfill the predictions he made for the uses of the phonograph in an article published in the *North American Review* (June 1878):

Letter writing and all kinds of dictation without the aid of a stenographer.

Phonographic books which will speak to blind people without effort on their part.

The teaching of elocution.

Reproduction of music.

The "Family Record"—a registry of sayings, reminiscences, etc., by members of a family in their own words, and of the last words of dying persons.

Music boxes and toys.

Clocks that should announce in articulate speech the time for going home, going to meals, etc.

The preservation of languages by exact reproduction of the manner of pronouncing.

Educational purposes such as preserving the explanations made by a teacher, so that the pupil can refer to them at any moment, and spelling or other lessons placed upon the phonograph for convenience in committing to memory.

Connection with the telephone, so as to make that instrument an auxiliary in the transmission of permanent and invaluable records, instead of being the recipient of momentary and fleeting communication.

Remarkable predictions, considering that Edison made them over a century ago. But, contrary to his hopes, the applications of the phonograph as a *recording* as well as a *listening* device were comparatively limited. Since record-cutting machines were large and costly, individuals rarely owned them. Not until the development of wire recording, shortly after World War II, did it become possible to make home recordings of fairly good quality at moderate cost. Soon after that, the new tape recorders brought home recording within everyone's reach. Today anyone who can afford a camera can afford a tape recorder. Tape is inexpensive. It can be used and reused almost indefinitely. Repeated playback does not decrease it usability. The ease with which we can edit tape makes possible a multitude of applications at low cost. For example, I used tape to create a two-minute sound portrait of my niece as she grew up over a period of twelve years. I could have compiled this portrait by using other media. I might have recorded her voice on optical motion-picture film over a period of twelve years, and then clipped, cut, and edited my film down to a two-minute presentation. But, unlike magnetic tape, optical film records the sound in visual form and it cannot be reused. My expenses over the period of twelve years would have run to some twenty thousand dollars.

By taping my sound portrait, the only real cost was the few feet of tape used in the final, two-minute version—a cost of approximately twenty cents. All the tape I used other than the tape for the final, two-minute version was mine to erase and use again for other projects. Note how this astonishing reduction in cost democratizes the process of recording.

Records, wax cylinders, and wire recorders, the predecessors of audiotape, did not lend themselves to editing. The usual procedure was to record a spoken or musical performance and then play back that recording, unedited, at a later moment. The recording re-created the time and space relationships that existed within the real event.

Audiotape makes it possible for us to edit a single song from many musical "takes" recorded at different times and places. The artist can manipulate his temporal-spatial relationships within the song during editing sessions. The final product is not a re-creation of a previous creative performance but, rather, a unique creation unto itself, an original performance. We can find similar temporal-spatial constructions in news programs, documentaries, and many interview shows. For instance, the single documentary that we see on television may have been constructed from many interviews that were recorded at different times in different locations, providing many hours of material that was finally edited down to one hour.

Because he can now manipulate time and space during editing, the artist is no longer confined within time and space boundaries. This has radically affected the expectations of audiences. They are less likely to compare media experience with everyday reality. In motion pictures, for instance, we accept the musical score that accompanies the action, although we live our real lives without such musical assistance. We may also see a close-up of an actor and hear him voice his thoughts although his lips do not move. Media experiences constitute a separate reality.

When radio and records offered copies or re-creations of a live performance, we felt that the live performance was clearly more "real" than the recording. But with audiotape's constructed reality there is no live performance of which the tape is a copy. And so a fascinating reversal has taken place: Concerts are now

often weak copies of tapes and records. The live performance cannot match the control or design structures made possible by tape, such as one person singing four parts. Thus, with the exception of the classical solo or symphonic concert, we may prefer the tape to real-life performance. At one time, we measured a recording against a live performance, and this formed the basis of our critical judgment. Now the tape has often become the actuality against which we measure the live performance. The tape has become an original.

The media have encouraged in us a growing preference for the new, constructed reality. So overpowering is our involvement with electronic media generally that a face-to-face encounter may seem unreal in relation to our electronic communication reality. When people meet a disc jockey or singer, his radio or recorded voice is the standard by which they judge him. They do not judge the media by the man; rather, they judge the man by media standards.

The reality of a tape can be so pervasive that it often carries more authority than firsthand witness. Remember how deeply the Patty Hearst tapes affected us when we first heard them? Even had they been counterfeit, they would have compelled a belief and inspired an emotional reaction. Print, unless constructed by a master, could not have affected us so deeply, and our feelings about Patty Hearst would have been different had we learned of her situation through letters.

We considered the Watergate tapes the essence of truth. Nixon himself knew that the tapes represented a reality more powerful than any transcripts of them or oral testimony about them. Nixon was afraid to let the public hear the tapes. He said correctly that out of context the tapes could distort the truth, but he was also aware that the truth would be impotent against the more powerful reality: the emotional impact of the spoken word.

The power of tape rests further in its ability to capture a moment and preserve it for all time. Even in the days of wax cylinders, people realized that recordings outlast live performances and inevitably reach a larger audience. In theory, the audience for any tape can be the entire world of today and the future. This gives great value to that preserved moment, and it inspires the performer to take special care in the performance. A singer who may not have been in good voice for one concert can comfort himself with the knowledge that his vocal cords will be in better condition for his next concert. But if he is not in good voice on a tape, he will not be in "good voice" for as long as that tape exists.

What are the implications of this for the everyday reality we live? Every time we look at a television program, we are involved with tape. The television news program is not a natural reality. It is a constructed reality. In many aspects of our lives the moment-to-moment reality is not as impressive as that constructed reality that can come to exist on tape. We adjust the everyday world to bring it in line with the needs of tape reality. Today news makers often try to make news rather than simply live it, or experience it. People who want news coverage for some activity design that activity to meet the needs of the newscasters. They might decide when and where to hold a rally in order to get the best coverage. The recording devices actually determine what is news. People will organize an event in such a way as to make it sound best on tape. It matters less how many people attend a rally or what they do there than what they sound like on the news and what the news commentators say about them. With portable recorders available everywhere, many people literally make their own news, cut it, edit it to a length stations generally use, and then distribute it to the media.

The Iranians gave us perhaps the best example of a group using media both to make news and control coverage. The mullahs, for all their alleged backwardness in other matters, proved to be highly sophisticated in their media manipulations. In Washington, pro-Khomeini officials kept their telephone lines to Teheran open. They also monitored American television day and night so that the mullahs knew what was going on here every minute. They were also aware of the significance of television ratings. That is doubtless why Khomeini gave more interview time to Mike Wallace's highly rated show "60 Minutes" than to NBC, ABC, or PBS. In the final moments of the hostage drama, Teheran practically dictated the news to the world.

Today people are less likely to think of tape or radio as a source of information. Someone may say, "Hey, I just heard a great new song!" He will not say that he heard it on radio, because he no longer conceives of the radio as a transmitter of an experience or a performance. Radio, tape, and records are now natural firsthand experiences in our homes, not devices for bringing in other environments.

Since the constructed piece of music on tape is the base reality against which we now measure live performance, the function and notoriety of designers who edit and produce records and tapes has grown significantly. Record critics are beginning

to deal with principles of sound design. Individual design styles have developed. Audiences are learning to appreciate creative mixes as well as creative performances. A few sound designers have even become stars. George Martin, the Beatles' producer who designed their hit albums, is an example. His name on any album has a sales value.

We can now manipulate time and space. Using audio- and videotape, we can record elements at different times in different places, then join them together to construct a temporal-spatial unit that exists on tape but has no counterpart in the tangible world. Yet, paradoxically, that temporal-spatial unit is very much a part of our new real world.

How Commercials
Work

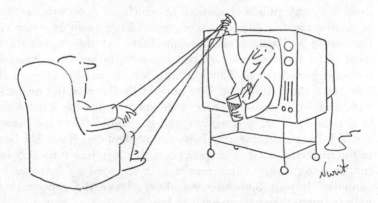

Except for an occasional Tupperware or Avon lady, the electronic media have practically eliminated door-to-door salespeople from American life. In their place we now have television and radio, which sit in almost every home in the country and sell a more varied line of goods than any salesperson could ever handle. While the individual traveling salesman had to depend on the appeal of his product and his personal gifts of persuasion, television and radio employ the best designers, advertising writers, actors, models, and spokesmen in the country for the job.

Radio and television convey to all people the emotionality, style, and quality that produce the best results. They standardize the technique of selling and affect people more deeply than most salesmen can. Today, many stores hire "sales" personnel primarily to write up orders, rather than to sell.

To a large extent, radio and television created the supermarket. A generation ago, people still patronized neighborhood
grocery stores. The shopkeeper stood behind a counter with his
back to shelves which displayed a selection of goods, while
many other items were kept in the rear storeroom. You went into
the store having memorized what you wanted, or else with a
shopping list. After you had checked off everything on your list,
the storekeeper might ask you if you had enough potatoes and
flour for the week, or point out some vegetables just come into
season. Today the supermarket has replaced the corner grocery.
The counter, the old shelves, and the grocer are gone. The store
itself is a large public stockroom in which an enormous variety
of products are on display. Commercials have made us aware of
the nature and names of these products. At the supermarket
most of us function with evoked memory, rather than learned
memory. For instance: This morning Johnny cut his finger and
you put a Band-Aid on it. You noticed that it was the next-to-
last Band-Aid in the box. Later in the day you see the Band-Aids
in the supermarket or drugstore and the sight evokes the memory of Johnny's cut finger and the almost depleted Band-Aid box
in the medicine chest. This process ends the reliance on lists or
simple rote memory. This results in a tremendous increase in
"impulse" buying. Somehow we always leave the supermarket
with far more than we expected to buy.

Years ago, the A & P piled foodstuffs in its display windows
to make customers aware of what products were available in the
store. Today television is the primary display window for most
consumer goods. Consequently, some new stores have been built
with no display windows whatsoever.

What accounts for the power and influence of electronic-
media commercials?

To understand how commercials work, it is necessary to leave
aside (at least for the moment) several catchphrases, e.g., commercials are stupid . . . condescending . . . annoying . . . extraordinary sales tools . . . powerful political weapons. All these
phrases and epithets are true for some commercials, but they do
not inform us about how commercials actually affect people.

Radio and television commercials can work in various ways.
Some clearly try to tell the viewer/listener about a product and

then sell it. In others, the telling and selling are a side effect of the commercial. One commercial may offer a product and carefully list the five colors in which it is available. You are expected to remember the five colors. Another commercial may rapidly list fifteen colors available for a product. The second commercial is not designed to make you remember the fifteen colors but only to get across the idea that the product is available in many colors.

Many people object to the number of electronic commercials that are broadcast. Yet, pick up a newspaper in practically any city in the United States and you will discover that the ratio of print ads to content in that paper is many times higher than the ratio of commercials to program content on radio or television. This being so, why are we more aware of electronic commercials than we are of print ads? In a newspaper, we only bother to read ads if they interest us. Otherwise, we simply turn the page or focus our attention on a news story. We hardly know the ad exists. On radio and television, however, we have no fast-forward button to speed us past the commercials. Even though we may mentally tune the commercial out, we know it's there and it gets in the way of the program material. Unless we go to the trouble of turning off the set or lowering the sound, we cannot skip the commercials.

Some commercials offend us by shouting at us and trying to pressure us into buying as we sit in our living room. The absence of information in some advertising sells more effectively than an abundance of explicit selling messages. I designed one such commercial for Bosco, a syrup used to make chocolate-milk drinks. The commercial said practically nothing about the product. It simply showed a jar of Bosco accompanied by the sound of a child eagerly chug-a-lugging it down in great gulps and then gasping for breath. A viewer who has had any experience with children knows that they do not gulp a drink down unless they like it very much. Without putting it into words, this commercial announced, "Children love Bosco!"

In commercials, lines can be spoken with the tonality and expressiveness we give to other words in order to evoke certain feelings. Imagine the voice of a worried mother saying to a child, "You don't feel well? Come to Mama." Using the same

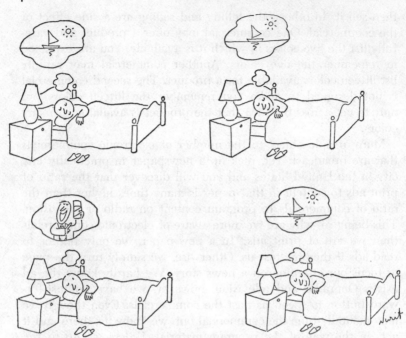

kind of voice and inflection, a commercial announcer might say, "Got a headache? Come to Bufferin." If the advertiser can evoke a connection between the relief a medicine might bring with the comfort most of us received from our mothers when we were children, the commercial will have power. In this way, commercials try to connect with built-in emotional signals stored in our brain. This is what enables the sound on radio and television to be "subliminal" in the sense that those whom it influences are unaware of the true source of that influence.

The most effective commercials do not tell us what to do or how to react. They present carefully chosen stimuli that evoke certain inner connections and elicit the desired behavior or reaction. A series of AT&T commercials provided a simple and effective example of this. The visual in these commercials showed people in close, warm, and loving association, family members, old and dear friends, as they talked to each other on the telephone. Over a recording of a song called "Feeling," the sound track conveyed the joy in the voices of the people as they talked by phone to loved ones far away. That's all. No one exhorted the listener to make a long-distance call. No one said, "Keep in touch by phone." The spots did not *direct* people to make long-distance calls. They made them *feel* like doing so.

A commercial can have extraordinary power when it makes people conclude that it is putting them in touch with a piece of reality. Such spots strike a responsive chord with the reality the listener or viewer has experienced. However, there is an important difference between the reality we experience in day-to-day life and the realism we *receive* during a radio or television commercial.

A series of radio commercials I prepared for American Airlines illustrates what is meant by a constructed reality. The series was called "Sounds of the Cities." We selected the ten American cities most frequently serviced by the airline and did three commercials on each one. These commercials utilized a concept that cities have a sound signature as well as a visual signature such as the Empire State Building in New York, San Francisco's Golden Gate Bridge, the Capitol or the White House in Washington. Every city has its own sound.

The best-known "Sounds of the Cities" spot was one that featured San Francisco. During the time I was working on the series, I was acquainted with a blind man known as Moondog who was a familiar character on New York City's streets. His usual haunt was the Avenue of the Americas in New York's midtown area. Moondog wore sandals and draped himself in a flowing garment with a leather thong belt, all homemade. He was bearded and he wore his hair long even in the days when the crewcut was standard. Moondog would materialize before the plaza of some new glass-walled skyscraper—and just stand there. Anyone who stopped to talk to him discovered that he could have an intelligent and involving conversation. Moondog wrote poetry and sold it to passersby. He was also a street musician and I later made several records of his music as he played it on the street.

Moondog and I both lived on the West Side. At about three o'clock in the morning of a foggy spring day my telephone rang. Moondog was calling to say, "Dig those crazy horns!" I listened. Through the windows of my home I could hear the groaning of

foghorns up and down the Hudson River. I immediately said to
Moondog, "How would you like to record your music against the
sound of the foghorns?"

He agreed. At four in the morning he arrived in my living
room carrying several handmade instruments of his own devis-
ing. The sound of one of the instruments was like the sound of
trolley-car bells. I went to the roof of my building to install a
microphone and then fed it back to a speaker in my living room
so that Moondog could hear it. The lonesome sound of the foghorns filled the room as Moondog played his instrument, and
what I had on tape was the "Sound of San Francisco"—trolley
bells clanging and drums beating against a background of foghorns. Thus I was able to construct a sound pattern that people
really felt was San Francisco. In fact, many have asked me in
what part of San Francisco I made that recording.

Various techniques in media advertising have changed the role
of what we call "product credibility," a phrase that describes
public confidence in a product. In the past, print ads never omitted the name of the manufacturer of the product. Coffee was not
just coffee. It was Maxwell House. An electronic product was a
Westinghouse. Chocolate was Nestlé's chocolate. Hair products
bore the name of Clairol. But in television today, a commercial
will tell us of an instant coffee called Taster's Choice, without
ever mentioning that The Nestlé Company manufactures it.
Taster's Choice suggests a product benefit, and the product
benefit becomes the name of the product. Another product-
benefit name for a hair preparation is Nice 'n' Easy. The name of
the maker of Nice 'n' Easy, Clairol Incorporated, is no longer an
important part of the television commercial, the product label,
or even the print ads.

Many advertisers and their agencies prepare inexpensive
rough versions of their commercials. These are called "animat-
ics," and they are used for testing purposes because they
generally cost only a fraction of the cost of the finished commercial. It's an inexpensive method of getting an indication of how a
spot will work. These roughs often have a spontaneity that is
lost when the agencies produce the finely finished and carefully
constructed commercial itself. These same advertisers and agencies are often surprised to discover that the roughs, with their

spontaneity, often test out better than the expensive, finished product. In a received medium like television, spontaneity, even with imperfections, is an asset, because it can connect with people's real-life experience. It is more important than perfection without spontaneity. In the more than twenty-five years that I have worked with sound for commercials, I have never made a single rough. All my takes have had the quality I wanted in the final product, and many times my first recordings capture the spontaneity I find so valuable.

Spontaneity adds believability. It is a special bonus I get when working with non-actors or people who really use a product. I don't employ amateurs exclusively, but most people who use a product really are amateurs, and their own feelings about that product are more genuine than the feelings that writers and actors put into commercials. Everybody automatically concludes that professional actors and actresses are paid to say what they say in commercials, and therefore they will say anything. The amateur says what he feels, and his livelihood does not depend on it. To ask amateurs to do retakes is to ask them to be actors, which they are not. I simply record them as they talk about the product, use it, or go through a situation related to it. But this concept of spontaneity goes against the grain of many trained actors and actresses. In the early 1950s I was asked to audition eight women for Birds Eye frozen foods. The agency wanted professional actresses and asked me to come to the agency office for a casting session. As each woman came in, I asked her a few simple questions, such as, "Do you do your own shopping?" "Where do you shop?" "What are your favorite foods?" I made my choice of women from those who could answer my questions easily and directly.

Later the agency told me it had received many complaints from the women who were not chosen. They were put off because no one gave them a script and no one asked them to "act." But I was not interested in either a script or acting. I was interested in a spontaneous response to simple questions.

When we were ready to shoot the commercial, the women we were using came dressed in their street clothes, but they carried with them the clothes they expected to change into. I didn't want them to change. They were dressed in the casual attire they usually wore when they went shopping, and that was exactly what I wanted. I closed down the dressing room and the makeup room and shot them just as they came to me. The result was an effective and believable commercial.

Believability is more important than startling effects. When Henry Ford II resigned from the Board of Trustees of the Ford Foundation, he got a few things off his chest. According to the New York *Times,* Ford was of the opinion that "Big business must come clean with the public and admit its mistakes and faults if it wants to repair its severely damaged credibility among consumers. . . ." Among the faults, Mr. Ford included inept advertising, and he referred to some of the Ford Motor Company ads in all media as "junk."

Ford ads strove to make the Ford automobile unique, but most people don't buy cars for uniqueness. They buy the model they believe will best fulfill the commonplace functions for which cars are intended: to drive to work, to school, to the hospital, to the supermarket. In a word, people want automobiles for basic transportation. When commercials try to make a car unique, they often do so in ways that are unbelievable or unimportant. Very few people are interested in going from a standstill to 90 miles per hour in a few seconds. An automobile may have a top speed of 140 miles per hour, but most of us are not interested in courting death. One car maker's commercial shows an automobile precariously perched atop a huge rock peak jutting up from a western desert, hardly an ordinary driving situation. Another shows a car driving out of the ocean.

Industry used to accept without question the hitherto sacrosanct "Unique Selling Proposition" (U.S.P.). U.S.P. is a kind of gentleman's agreement preventing any two companies from making the same product claim in an advertisement. The electronic media, however, have stripped all the value from the concept of U.S.P.

It is impossible to determine what is true and what is false in a print advertisement. If five camera companies make the same claim in print advertisements, each one has a 20-percent chance of being perceived as telling the truth. If these five companies all make different claims, they bring their chance of being perceived as telling the truth up to 50 percent. The reader simply will or will not believe each company's particular claim. The sound or look of sincerity, and many other emotional stimuli present in electronic media commercials, are absent from print ads. Because we cannot tell truth from falsity in print alone, print is the only medium that is divided into categories labeled "fact" and "fiction."

Since you *feel* quality that can affect you emotionally in radio and television commercials, U.S.P. is no longer necessary. If each of the five camera companies retains a different announcer to read the same commercial, listeners will tend to identify and react more favorably to one of them because of the manner of his presentation, belief in his sincerity, and other factors that cannot be precisely measured.

Once I get a good announcer, I let him think for himself. I only tell him what I want him to make me feel, not what he should do. Then I let him know when I feel it from him and when I don't. Even when announcers are reading directly from a script, they have to read as though they were talking to you alone, even if millions of people are listening to them.

Credibility in electronic media comes mainly from how the commercial makes you *feel*. In fact, an inferior commercial may discourage you from buying a product produced by a company in which you previously had confidence. The company whose commercial makes you feel the same thing more deeply than the commercial of a rival company is the one that comes out on top.

One oil company may promise that their gasoline will clean your engine, but listeners don't believe that claim. When they want their engines cleaned, they still go to the garage to get the job done. Another gas company may promise more mileage, but listeners know that what will really give them more mileage is a smaller car. Claims such as these are not perceivable or believable. People buy gasoline to make their cars go. There was no gasoline advertising during the gas shortage, and yet the companies maintained their consumers. There has been very little gas advertising since then, but people continue to buy gas.

A common charge made against commercials and the entire advertising community is that they attempt to sell products that are superfluous or inferior. In an article called "Tomorrow: The Republic of Technology," published in a special issue of *Time*

(Jan. 17, 1977), Daniel J. Boorstin wrote, "We will be misled if we think that technology will be directed primarily to satisfy 'demands' or 'needs' or to solving recognized 'problems.' There was no 'demand' for the telephone, the automobile, radio, or television." He continues by remarking that "technology is a way of multiplying the unnecessary," and he concludes this section of his essay with the statement "Working together, technology and advertising create progress by developing the need for the unnecessary."

There's enough truth in Boorstin's critique to make it enticing, but not enough knowledge of technology and advertising to make it totally valid. It's true that before the telephone, radio, and automobile were invented, people did not feel a specific need for those devices. However, they did feel the need for improved communication, more-accessible entertainment, and swifter transportation, and they felt that need in emotional terms. "Oh, how I wish I could talk to my brother up in Canada!" "Oh, how I wish I could hear Caruso in Chicago tonight!" "Oh, how I wish it didn't take me so awfully long to get to work every day!"

Sophisticated and effective commercials can sell inferior products only on a very short-term basis.

Some years ago, the late great animator John Hubley did an exquisite series of television commercials for a new cereal. Many people responded to these masterful commercials by buying a package of this cereal, but very few bought a second package. People simply didn't like it. A year or two later, Hubley did a second series, of equally brilliant commercials, for the same company, and with the same results.

When people find that a commercial has misrepresented an inexpensive product, they tend not to buy it again. When a product is quite expensive, factors other than the commercial enter into the buying decision. Potential customers will first check with experts or with people who have used the product. Hardly anyone will buy an automobile on the basis of a commercial. The function the commercial serves is to make potential customers keep in mind the particular make of automobile it is promoting, because automobile buyers almost always comparison-shop before making their decision.

Marshall McLuhan made the astute observation that "people tend to read ads for things they already own." They also watch and listen to commercials for things they already own. When a new product comes along, people can't identify with it unless they see it in relation to something familiar. Let's say that someone invents an all-year automobile tire whose tread gives as much traction on ice as on asphalt. A commercial for such a tire might begin by asking the auto owner, "Are you sick of changing to snow tires every winter?" A consumer who can identify the tires he has yet to buy with the tires he owns will probably be influenced by such an approach.

No matter how hard an advertiser tries, he can't sell products for which people feel no emotional or physical need, nor can he sell a product that people feel is obsolete. Folklore has it that the public-relations man Jim Moran sold an icebox to an Eskimo, but could he sell ten iceboxes to ten Eskimos year after year? Many products have had very short lives although well-funded advertising campaigns promoted them. This is especially noticeable in the cosmetics field.

The electronic commercial as we know it began with radio in the 1930s and '40s, when the radio network systems were at their peak. Advertisers saw radio as a medium that could reach large numbers of people quickly for quick results. (The Jack Benny Sunday-night show made Jell-O and its "six delicious flavors" known to everyone in the country.) Networks were the most efficient and fastest way to distribute national programs. Satellites, which can do the same job, were not yet in existence.

When television came along, the role of radio networks diminished. Television networks took over and became the major area of entertainment. Television networks, which enable millions of people everywhere in our country to see and hear the same material at the same moment, are still the best source of common instant information. Just as the automobile forced a new role upon the horse and carriage, television forced a new role upon radio. Radio fell into second place and took on a new function, that of a highly specialized local service. Today the old radio networks as they originally existed have all but disappeared (with the exception of a few news and special-interest national radio networks). In their place local special-interest radio has emerged. As a consequence, radio commercials have become more of an exact science. An advertiser who uses radio and television is interested only in that part of the audience that has a need for his product or may become interested in it. To this end, he studies the distribution pattern of his product, selects stations that can reach his potential audience in that distribution area, and tries to determine the most cost-effective way of doing this.

One of the most fruitful uses of radio, from an advertiser's standpoint, is narrowcasting (as opposed to broadcasting). For instance, if we want to reach the elderly, we buy time on Station A. We reach teenagers on Station B, young blacks on Station C, Hispanics on Station D, classical music lovers on Station E, jazz buffs on Station F, news hounds on Station G. Analyzing an audience along a different dimension, we may learn that 69 percent of Station H's listeners read the *Daily News*, while 65 percent of Station I's listeners read the New York *Times*. During the morning, 80 percent of Station J's listeners are in their cars, most of them driving to work.

In Massachusetts a number of large companies felt that it was getting too expensive to do business there. They believed that a more efficient handling of state funds could provide the same services while reducing the cost of government for themselves and other taxpayers. We prepared a series of radio commercials aimed at the state legislators. Here is one of them:

> Massachusetts has the kind of climate that invites people to swim in the summertime, ski in the wintertime, and pack up and leave at tax time. Oh, we used to be careful about the way our taxes were spent, and companies and people liked it here, didn't feel squeezed for money. States determine their own climate of competition, and the Massachusetts climate says, "Expensive." Let's do something about that. Join us. Paid for by Citizens for Economy in Government.

These commercials were run over an eight-month period, and millions heard them. Yet the people we were really aiming at were the state legislators, since they alone could do something about the problem. The rest of our audience was just "listening in." The commercials succeeded. The next Massachusetts budget was a more rational document, and the companies that organized the campaign remained in the state.

Narrowcasting was employed in a series of help-wanted commercials for Bamberger's chain of department stores, in New Jersey. Bamberger's wanted to advertise job opportunites at a new branch they were opening. Before designing the commercial, we interviewed the best and most productive Bamberger's employees, almost all of whom were women, to find out what had impelled them to look for work, why they chose Bamberger's, what they enjoyed most about their jobs. We also asked what radio stations they listened to, and when they listened. We discovered that before going to work for Bamberger's most of the employees fell into one or more of the following categories:

· Women whose children had recently left home.
· Women with time on their hands.
· Women who felt they had "something to contribute" but no outlet for their skills.
· Women who wanted to meet new people, even on a casual basis.
· Women who found shopping enjoyable and who felt a sense of accomplishment when they helped other people shop.

The store's flexible work schedules attracted many of them who had domestic schedules to meet. Some, though not all, needed an extra paycheck, but even those who had other means of support enjoyed their increased financial freedom.

Here is part of the radio spot we designed:

Well, what are you going to do with yourself now that the kids are all grown up and gone? Wouldn't it be fun to go out and meet new people, maybe even start working again? You've got a lot to contribute. And an extra paycheck could go a long way. You know, there's a new department store opening in September at the Lehigh Valley Mall. Bamberger's. And they really do need people like you. People who like to shop and who like to help other people shop. And Bamberger's will have so many different work schedules—mornings, afternoons, evenings, full time, part time, weekdays, Saturdays, and they'll have employee discounts and nice benefits, too. You know, Bamberger's really appreciates people like you, people who care and try. So you probably won't stay at your starting salary very long.

We did not aim this commercial at anyone who was listening to just any radio station. Armed with the results of our presearch, the commercial was narrowcast to women who were actively looking for a way to adjust to some change in their lives or status. Presearch had also told us which radio stations had the best chance of reaching such women. When they heard the commercial, they felt we were speaking directly to them, that we understood them and their problems. Later, in describing those who answered the commercial, an executive of Bamberger's said, "We couldn't have done any better if we had knocked on the doors of exactly the kind of people we wanted."

I believe that the best commercials nearly always make people feel that the advertiser is talking directly to them. It is easy to understand what engenders that feeling. Radio and television advertisers rely heavily on research. They know exactly how people feel about a product they want to advertise, what questions they have in relation to it, their estimate of its efficacy, to what extent they truly need it, their social involvement and experience with it. Commercials, being a product of this research, are inherently a form of narrowcasting.

In rare cases, commercials and research can center on one or two people. This is the most finely honed narrowcasting of all. I once produced a campaign for a radio network designed to reach and influence the president of a major automobile company who didn't believe in using radio to sell cars. The purpose of this campaign was to change his mind and induce him to see to it that his company advertised on radio during "drive time," when people drive to and from work, usually with their radios playing.

We wanted to research the president to discover what his interests were. We found out what radio station he listened to during the time he was in his car driving to work, what newspapers he read, what magazines he subscribed to. (We did this by including him in a group of fifty businessmen in the area whom we interviewed about current government and business problems. We told them that their names and their answers to our questions would be made public. None of them objected to this.)

We designed radio commercials specifically to influence him.

These commercials talked about automobiles. Since automobiles
were his business, he listened. The major theme of the commercials was that people think more consciously about automobiles when they are driving automobiles. Obviously, thousands
of other people heard those commercials, but we were talking
to only one man. He listened because we discussed *his* concerns,
his aims, *his* problems. He must have felt these commercials
were talking to him, even though it probably never entered
his head that he was the only person we were interested in
talking to. The spots we used said not one word about buying
air time on the station that retained me. They only asked if it
didn't make sense to talk to people about automobiles when
they were *in* their automobiles, driving to and from work.

We knew the commercials reached him, because they contained a phone number. His auto company used that phone
number when someone called the station to buy many thousands
of dollars' worth of time. Incidentally, six other companies with
which we were unacquainted also used that phone number to
buy radio time.

In a similar campaign, and for similar reasons, I designed a
narrowcast aimed at the president of a pharmaceutical company
that is a major producer of dental supplies. The objective was to
get his company to advertise in a dental magazine that distrib-
utes free copies to the profession. Ostensibly, our campaign was
aimed only at dentists. Almost every spot started with the simple
question "Are you a dentist?" Then it went on to tell dentists
how much they could learn about new products and techniques
by reading a copy of the dental magazine that was waiting for
them in their offices. The spots left the impression that dentists
were relying more and more on this particular magazine for
news of important professional developments.

The president of the pharmaceutical company, whom we had
researched just as we had researched the automobile president,
apparently heard the commercials. Although the spots had not
attempted to sell advertising space in the dental magazine, the
pharmaceutical company soon jumped in and bought space on a
long-term basis.

Some commercials that promote huge conglomerates are another kind of narrowcasting. TRW, for instance, advertises on

both radio and television. The commercials tell of the many impressive industrial developments in which TRW is engaged. Yet TRW makes no product the average television viewer is likely to buy, nor is it trying to sell one. Why, then, does the company run television commercials?

TRW is trying to build confidence among its stockholders and encourage others to become stockholders, though it can do so only indirectly, because selling stocks on television is illegal. But TRW doesn't need to tell the viewer to buy stock. The commercials are designed to make the viewer think of it himself when he becomes aware of the company's vast and successful industrial enterprises. The extent of these enterprises gives credibility to the stock.

Media commercials sell products, change behavior, elect politicians, influence your choice of college, determine the entertainment you see, the sports events you attend, the shoes you wear, and the gum you chew. And while they do all this to you, you think they're doing it to the other people.

The John Jay Campaign: A Case Study

In March 1976 I awoke one morning to hear on the radio that New York's Board of Higher Education had voted ten to one to close the John Jay College of Criminal Justice, a branch of the City University. I knew Richard Ward, the college's acting vice-president. At that time the acting president and vice-president of John Jay were interim appointees, filling in until such time as the Board of Higher Education selected a new administration. John Jay College is almost directly across the street from my house and studio, and after I heard the report I walked over to discuss the news with Dick Ward. I suggested that we form a committee including Dick, myself, my wife, and a few other people who were interested in saving the institution. I would take care of the media on a volunteer basis and Dick would take charge of raising money for the campaign. We shook hands on the proposal and got to work.

I called Richard Dresner, a friend of mine who heads Richard Dresner Associates, a public-opinion-research firm, and he volunteered to take a poll to determine what attitudes and beliefs people held relative to institutions such as John Jay. With the help of students at John Jay and the firm's telephone polling system, he got the results of the poll in a few days. We learned how people felt about the City University system, crime, John Jay College itself, and the effectiveness of then-Mayor Abe Beame and Governor Hugh Carey in controlling crime.

The poll produced some interesting results. In terms of the services people expected from city government, they considered police protection the most important. Fire protection came next, followed by higher education and sanitation. Almost all the respondents regarded higher education as the key to better jobs. This suggested that New Yorkers would be sympathetic to saving John Jay College, since it could be perceived as an institution that was attempting to solve two of the problems to which they gave high priority: crime and education. We also discovered that most people believed that both the mayor and the governor were inadequate when it came to dealing with the problems of urban crime. This presearch told us what to do.

Our committee sent copies of the poll and our analysis to a number of key political figures both in the city and in Washington: councilmen, borough presidents, congressmen, and senators. Once they'd gone over this material, about half of them wrote or called in to express their support. I also sent the material to Mike O'Neill, the editor of the *Daily News,* who happened to be a client of mine at the time. While he couldn't give us an editorial, he did offer us space on the Op-Ed Page. Gerry Lynch, the acting president of John Jay College, wrote an article in defense of the school, and the *Daily News* published it a few days before the Board of Higher Education was to vote on the issue again.

The research material we'd gathered engendered some stories and a few editorials in publications other than the *Daily News,* including the New York *Times.* WCBS-TV broadcast an editorial supporting the decision to close the school, and this caused a small hassle. Then Gerry Lynch, in accordance with WCBS-TV policy, asked for and was granted time to broadcast a rebuttal in the form of an editorial reply. WCBS said they would first have to approve that editorial reply. Our position was that while WCBS certainly had the right to demand proof of the legitimacy of anyone who replies to an editorial, since they are obligated to keep the airwaves free of cranks and crackpots, in no way did we concede their right to approve the answer. The network was obdurate about this. Then I told them that if they did not give Gerry Lynch a free hand with his editorial reply, I would buy air time and openly discuss WCBS's policy in that regard. I strongly believe that a network does not have the right to censor the content of what people want to say in their own defense once the station has attacked them or their beliefs. WCBS finally agreed to let Gerry Lynch say whatever he wanted about the situation, but the station allowed him to do only one take of the two-minute reply, refusing him the courtesy of polishing up a little roughness here and there. Ironically, Gerry Lynch broadcast a very effective editorial reply and it all came out well for us.

Our commercials went after individual members of the Board of Higher Education. The approach I wanted to use was to embarrass them among their peers and their friends. I wanted people who knew them personally to confront board members about their decision to close the college. One commercial focused on Robert Kibbee, chancellor of the City University:

> Lots of people talk about crime. But is anyone doing anything about it? One man is. Robert Kibbee, chancellor of the City University. But you won't believe what he's doing about crime. He's planning to close John Jay College of Criminal Justice, where over four thousand of our policemen get advanced training. Governor Carey, if you're listening to this, please stop Chancellor Kibbee. One word from you can. Keep John Jay College open. . . . Paid for by Concerned Citizens Who Support John Jay College of Criminal Justice.

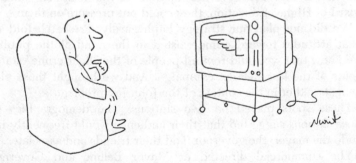

To understand the effect of a commercial like this on an individual, imagine yourself to be the chancellor of the City University. Then imagine hearing a commercial that refers to you by name and tells the whole world—it would seem like the whole world to you—that you are trying to destroy an institution that is dedicated to fighting crime.

We directed another commercial at Mayor Beame and Governor Carey:

This is a personal message for Mayor Beame and Governor Carey. When you were running for office, remember, you promised the people to fight crime, but now an unbelievable thing is happening that threatens our protection from crime: The Board of Higher Education is planning to close the John Jay College of Criminal Justice, the one college in New York that directly fights crime by giving training to over four thousand of the policemen we still have left. Now, Mayor Beame and Governor Carey, we've had too much experience with government officials who remain silent on important issues. We gave you political power to use for people. Now's the time to use it and show us that you meant what you said about fighting crime. Speak to the members of the Board of Higher Education that you both appointed and tell them that you want John Jay, the best crime-fighting college in the country, kept open.

These commercials had three objectives: to connect with an existing public attitude about crime; to recall public statements by government officials committing them to a certain position; and to create an atmosphere of shame about the current behavior of those officials, behavior which belied their promises. Since the mayor and the governor appointed the members of the Board of Higher Education, they could put pressure on them.

We did not plan our strategy haphazardly. Presearch told us what attitudes toward crime existed in the mind of the public. We knew that we could remind people of the "fight crime" statements of the last election campaign. And we brought those elements together in the context of the John Jay problem.

These spots played on two stations. The demographics of those stations suggested that their audience would frequently include the mayor, the governor, and their friends and associates.

The commercial directed at Mayor Beame and Governor Carey must have hit many sensitive spots, for within one hour of the first broadcast of that commercial a deputy mayor came to see me and said, "I've got to get that commercial off the air." Then he asked, "What are you going to the defense of this school for? It's only a bunch of dumb Irish cops." Hardly a classy argument, and he compounded his obtuseness by adding that the students weren't worth bothering about, since they had no community base and therefore lacked political clout. He didn't realize that as long as the media could rally support for them in all the boroughs of the city, the students did indeed have political clout.

The next day, Governor Carey sent an emissary to me with the same message: I must take my commercial off the air. I called my friend Joe Napolitan, the political campaign adviser and analyst, and said, "Joe, should I take it off the air?" Joe said, "Will they shoot you if you don't?" When I expressed doubts that Governor Carey would shoot me, he said, "Then, leave it on."

Earlier, when I had learned that the governor's emissary was coming to see me, I called Gerry Lynch, at John Jay. He told me that the governor's man had attended every meeting of the Board of Higher Education when the Board was discussing the proposal to shut down John Jay. When the man came to see me, he blandly announced that the governor had nothing whatever to do with the John Jay decision. I then told him that I knew he had attended every board meeting when it had John Jay on the agenda.

To mobilize public support, we created a series of radio commercials which featured members of the public. In one, a policeman who was a student at John Jay at the time spoke without a prepared script:

> Well, I've been attending John Jay College now for five years, full-time. I work full-time for the Police Department. And I'll have a B.S. in Criminal Justice. And you're not so narrow-minded as you were before you went to school, and being a cop, it's a great help out in the street, especially in the ghetto, where I work. You don't fly off the handle as easily as you had before. You find that there are other people and they have different cultures.

Let me emphasize that the policeman himself, not a trained announcer, recorded this commercial, and he projected sincerity and spontaneity, because he believed in every word he said.

In another commercial, we used a policeman and his wife:

Wife

My husband's a police officer.

Cop

I work in the 73rd Precinct, Brownsville.

Wife

For the past five years he's been attending John Jay College.

Cop

I'll have a B.S. in Criminal Justice.

Wife

Just recently we heard that they're closing down the school, and this is upsetting us all greatly.

Cop

First they take my buddies at work, and now they'll be taking my school.

Wife

All the policemen left need the school.

Cop

People are concerned about policemen being laid off. They should be just as concerned about the training the police officer gets at John Jay.

An announcer followed this message with details of the training and services that John Jay provides.

My wife, speaking as an educator and citizen, recorded this commercial:

My name is Reenah Schwartz and I live in Manhattan. I want to speak out publicly about something that's outrageous. The chancellor of the Board of Higher Education—Robert Kibbee is his name—is proposing to close John Jay College of Criminal Justice, and I just get damned angry when a public official like Mr. Kibbee keeps putting peace with politicians ahead of what the people need. John Jay is a school that trains policemen and firemen. We need John Jay. It's bad enough to cut the number of policemen and firemen, but now you want to cut the quality of those we still have. Enough is enough. As an educator, as a person who lives and works in New York, don't fool around with our lives. You make those cuts somewhere else, Mr. Kibbee. Keep John Jay.

In another commercial, we suggested that the continued existence of John Jay was of concern far beyond the borders of New York City:

My name is Walter Gavin, and I'm a detective superintendent in one of the largest provincial police forces in England, the Merseyside District. In fact, at the moment I'm representing the National Police College, in England. I have heard that John Jay College, which is well known to us over in England, is going to be closed. I just cannot believe that the proposal is receiving any serious consideration. We over in England have heard a considerable amount about John Jay. So much so that we are now exchanging professors between our college here and John Jay. This isn't something that we do lightly. In fact, we don't carry out any exchange system with any other college anywhere in the world. We think it would be a crime to close John Jay.

All these commercials, except for the one my wife recorded, were spontaneous. The people spoke from their hearts and not from prepared scripts, and they communicated their emotional involvement with the school. After the English police officer's commercial was broadcast, Gerry Lynch, the acting president of John Jay, told me that at one board meeting he heard talk to the effect that "Scotland Yard has come out for John Jay!"

Eventually, we won this campaign. One month after its inception, the Board of Higher Education did a complete about-face and voted unanimously (with one member absent) to keep John Jay open. Then Dick Ward sent me the following letter:

Dear Tony:

In discussing some of the effects of the John Jay campaign to save the College several facts come to mind which I'm sure you'll be interested in. While the primary goal of the campaign was to save the College, which was accomplished magnificently, there have been several side benefits.

First has been the impact of the radio campaign in generating widespread recognition of the College among the general public. When the decision to close John Jay was made, a poll revealed that less than five percent of the public knew the College existed. When the final vote was taken [by the Board of Higher Education—T.S.] a follow-up survey revealed that more than 80 percent of the public knew the College by name. This level of recognition has created a group of supporters who display a continued interest in the College and its mission.

Perhaps more important has been the direct benefit achieved through an increase in the number of applicants for admission to the College. Some 1,300 potential students have applied for admission to the College in the Fall. This is an increase of almost 500

over last year. If all of these students show up, and we are funded
at the present level, our budget should be increased by approximately $600,000.

There has also been an increase in the number of individuals
who attend College-sponsored functions, and this too has proved
beneficial in helping develop programs which are not funded
through the University.

When one considers that the primary thrust of the campaign
began with spots on two radio stations, WMCA and WQXR, and
looks at the resultant publicity, which has created so many side
effects, it is obvious that the media campaign was certainly cost-
effective. Our media expenditures amounted to less than $20,000
and if we realize even a $100,000 increase in the budget I would
have to say the campaign was fiscally successful. As you know, we
did not use tax-levied money for this campaign, so it can be viewed
as doubly successful.

Chancellor Kibbee turned out to be quite open and not at all
personally put off by the campaign we had waged. When I met
with him later, I asked if I could record his reaction to the campaign for the school's archives and, being at heart an educator,
he agreed. In our conversation he said:

Well, there were the normal kinds of things that happen. First, a
lot of mail started coming in, saying you have to save John Jay and
tying it up with criminal justice, saying we need protection and
you're doing away with everything we need most. Then we got a
lot of phone calls. Then I saw around my own office building people wearing SAVE JOHN JAY buttons, my own staff, too. Little incidents like the cab driver. I called a cab and got in a cab in front of
the Higher Education Building, and we hardly got away from the
curb when he asked me what's going to happen to John Jay. I was
a little flabbergasted because I didn't know it had gotten to the cab
drivers yet.

During the campaign, there was a tendency on the part of
some people at John Jay not to attack or embarrass members of
the Board of Higher Education, whose votes they were trying to
influence. I know from experience that such fears are groundless
in media campaigns. Appeasement never works. If you show
your opponents you have media clout, you win their respect.
The Board of Higher Education responded to Gerry Lynch's

fight for the schools by nominating and approving him as the president, and after the campaign Governor Carey appointed Gerry Lynch to head up his commission on gambling. And because we attacked with no legitimate holds barred, John Jay's position in the City University system is relatively secure.

And Now— the News!

On Thursday, May 22, 1980, professional baseball players were threatening a strike. At 6 A.M. the next day I woke up, turned my bedside radio to the New York all-news station, WINS, and learned that the players and owners had settled the dispute. Later that morning, I went out to buy the New York *Times* and the *Daily News*. The headline on the *Daily News* read: BASE-BALL FACES WALKOUT TODAY.

The following day, the *Daily News* carried a column in which writer Val Adams informed us that we have more than 456 million radio sets in the United States and the average American household has 5.7 radios.

To me, these two stories are interrelated. The term "newspaper" came into existence when newspapers were the major source of news and kept their readers as current as possible. Today newspapers can no longer do that, because the dissemination of news by radio and television is an instantaneous process, whereas newspapers have to be written, edited, printed, distributed, and sold before readers can learn the news. Until newspapers examine carefully their new contextual relationship to other media, they will not be as useful to their readers as they might be.

The dissemination of news by the electronic media has had a significant effect on newspapers in particular and on society in general. The newsboys who once used to peddle extra editions, hurriedly published to record some startling new development, have disappeared. The news "scoop," once the pride of the enterprising journalist, is now an extremely rare phenomenon. (Do young people today know the meaning of the word "scoop" as applied to journalism?) The circulation of many large newspapers has dropped sharply. Many children show a general lack of interest in reading, and many adults have stopped reading newspapers. Since newspapers can no longer be first with the news, they are giving more prominence to background and investigative journalism, special features, and op-ed pages, which offer comment and analysis rather than news itself. The news on radio or television makes the front page of the morning's newspaper almost obsolete.

On television, people see and hear current events as they are happening. Radio and television stations interrupt scheduled programs (but not commercials) to inform listeners of any important news development. In the last fifteen years, many radio stations have converted into all-news stations that broadcast twenty-four hours a day. In June 1980, Atlanta's Cable News Network, operating twenty-four hours a day, initiated a national service featuring news and special reports. In its very first week of existence, this network was already beating out the regular network news programs with live, on-the-spot coverage of news events as they were happening. Unfortunately, rather than using all the potential that electronic news-gathering and editing offer, most of the news that radio and television broadcast is written and read, and it comes from the same source that the newspapers use: the wire services.

In most network news programs, the local outlets of the network provide and broadcast segments of local news, whereas the Cable News Network, as of this moment, picks up news from all over but broadcasts the same news to everyone. It is not geared to distributing the local news to various urban and rural areas of the country.

Today a majority of the peoples of the world can learn of important news events within hours or even minutes. Before the electronic transmission of news, most people learned of political corruption long after the politician involved had finished his term of office or even his political career. Today that knowledge can reach us so swiftly that it can force his resignation from office and end his political career. As a result, many people believe that our era is one of unusually great corruption, but what impresses us as greater corruption is in reality our new electronic awareness of the corruption that has always existed. The same is true of crime and violence. We forget that in the late-eighteenth century men feared to walk the streets of Philadelphia alone at night and Victorian England was notorious for its nocturnal cutthroats.

People who live in areas of the country that have no media coverage find that their lives lack any real identity on television. Consider New Jersey, a state with no television of its own. The only New Jersey television programs are seen and heard on New York or Philadelphia stations, and consist of public-service programs, commissioners' reports, or political discussions whenever November draws near. The three commercial network affiliates cover no regular New Jersey news unless the event affects New York or Philadelphia, barring, of course, spectacular events like the flooding of huge parts of the state or a catastrophic gas storage-tank explosion. People in New Jersey never receive the kind of coverage of everyday news that the New Yorker or the Philadelphian takes for granted. As far as New Jersey is concerned, the news event is either earth-shaking or nonexistent.

This creates a peculiar phenomenon. People in outlying areas perceive as their own problems the problems of the major cities where the networks have facilities. When urban riots were breaking out all over the country, research indicated that people in non-urban areas were worried about the same problems that city people were trying to deal with, problems covered by local and national television. In such states as Utah, the people wrestled with urban concerns that were not really theirs. They tried to deal with the problems they encountered via the media, rather than with the reality of their own lives. Further, the depth of their concern with those problems was in exact proportion to the amount of media coverage, and similar to the concern of the urban dwellers.

One effect of the broad electronic news coverage available today is that most people share a vast amount of knowledge about current events. Unhappily, this knowledge is seldom knowledge in depth. The average 15- or 20-minute newscast does not contain as much solid information as we can glean from one page of a good newspaper.

People often comment that most of the news we hear today is bad news. The plain truth is that most "good" news bores us unless it is some highly dramatic development like the discovery of a cure for cancer. News of a bumper wheat crop in the Midwest will make us yawn, but if flood, drought, frost, or tornadoes ruin that crop, we will sit up and take notice. Of course we all know when the War of 1812 started, but how many of us know when it ended? After all, the end, rather than the beginning, of that war was the good news. If assassins seriously wound a prominent personality, it may be the first item on the news, but when he recovers and leaves the hospital, it will be the last item, unless he happens to be the President of the United States.

In some areas, the good news and the bad news come together. This is true of sports, politics, and war. These areas involve conflict: winners and losers. News of these conflicts is good news for those who support the winners, and bad news for those who support the losers. We might say that commercials are good news. They tell us of new products, improvements in existing products, and special sales. The bad news, of higher prices for these products, comes to us in the regular newscast, not in the commercials.

A newspaper reader constructs his own newspaper. He may glance at the headlines first, turn to a story on an inside page, peruse the comics, then digest the financial page or read a favorite sports columnist. But when he listens to news on radio or television he has no control over the order of the news, no fast-forward or rewind device. He has to take it in as it comes out of the faucet. This gives rise to one of the great fears of the networks and stations: that a specific item will bore a listener/viewer, who might then turn to another station or channel. Fewer listener/viewers means that the advertising rates on that station will go down. As a result, stations and networks organize the news in such a way as to guarantee the largest audience. They are more interested in holding a large audience that is satisfied with the headline aspects of a news event than in a smaller audience that wants an in-depth understanding of the story. Since commercials determine the income of a station or network, and the size of the audience determines the cost of those commercials, news programs often use a news item as a teaser to hold that audience. For instance, David Marash, a reporter for CBS local news in New York City, described the news stories that would come after a series of commercials. He told his audience that a "well-known Broadway producer stands indicted in an $800,000 swindle." Marash, of course, knew who that well-known Broadway producer was, but by making us play a guessing game rather than telling us, he was concealing the news so that we would "stay tuned." On WABC-TV, I heard the announcement "New York political giant dies of heart attack. Full details on the eleven o'clock 'Eyewitness News.'" I turned off WABC-TV, turned on the news station WINS, and learned that the political giant was Jim Farley. WABC-TV's failure to identify him was, again, a "tease" designed to make us "stay tuned."

One incident vividly illustrates how the networks pander to the mass audience in matters of news as well as in other programing so as not to lower the price tag on commercial time. In May 1977, on the "Today" show, NBC presented, live, Senator Proxmire and others who came to discuss national defense against atomic attack. They examined the possibility of an atomic-protection program and the activities of the atomic powers in this area. Then they assessed the probability of atomic attacks against this country. What these experts thought of the problems and possibilities of nuclear warfare certainly constituted legitimate news.

As they were discussing this, and just as Senator Proxmire was about to analyze the CIA's thinking on this subject, the announcer interrupted to say he was sorry but the network was going to cut away so the viewers could watch (live) Seattle Slew, the Kentucky Derby winner, wake up the morning after his triumph.

Now, which story has more meaning to our lives? Assessments of the world's precarious atomic position? A horse waking up? (The latter would have been news only if Seattle Slew did *not* wake up.)

In June 1980, former U. S. Attorney General Ramsey Clark went to a conference in Iran against the advice of his government. For a week he was a major news story, and he left Iran with firsthand information about the situation there. On June 9, Tom Brokaw held a first live interview from Paris with Ramsey Clark on NBC's "Today" show. Clark gave us his evaluation of the political situation in Iran. He told how the Iranian Government felt about our support of a monarch who they believed had murdered thousands of their people, and provided valuable insights about the hostages and about the political and social atmosphere in Iran at the time.

In the midst of this important interview that gave some depth to radio and television's headline reporting from Iran, Tom Brokaw interrupted Mr. Clark's answer to a question, saying he was sorry but he had to cut Mr. Clark off because he had run out of time.

NBC cut to a Tic Tac commercial.

The positive side to electronic-media news broadcasts is their ability to inform the world instantaneously about developments that affect all the people of the world. The negative side is the determination to please commercial time buyers by keeping the news "entertaining" at any cost, resulting in a tendency to make the size of the audience more important than the significance of the news.

Television has come to play an ever greater role as an intermediary in international as well as national affairs. When President Anwar Sadat made his historic flight from Cairo to the Ben-Gurion Airport, in Israel, to meet Prime Minister Menachem Begin, he had with him three ambassadors-at-large who had superseded our State Department: Barbara Walters, John Chancellor, and Walter Cronkite. President Sadat had no hesitation in using them as carrier pigeons for his views on the Middle East peace talks.

Of course, newsmen from the press, radio, and television have long been involved in international affairs. For instance, an ABC reporter acted as liaison man and held behind-the-scenes meetings in the Cuban missile crisis. But such involvements were then very hush-hush. Today television is a publicly acknowledged platform for the statesmen of the world. During Sadat's visit to Jerusalem none of the speeches he and the Israelis made in the Knesset were directed solely to the people in the hall. Sadat, Begin, and Peres were keenly aware of their worldwide television audience, and it was to that audience that they spoke.

This development has some disturbing aspects, particularly because these network "ambassadors" were not able to step out of their celebrity-commentator role: Barbara Walters' interview with Sadat was widely advertised before the event and covered more comprehensively than his appearance before the Knesset. The networks' values color not only our own perception of events but to a large extent influence which events take place and how they take place. The Roger Mudd interview at the beginning of Senator Ted Kennedy's 1980 campaign for the presidency did much to undercut that candidacy.

These ventures into television statesmanship raise some questions about the role of the networks. The networks' response to any and all questions about their values and actions is quite simple: freedom of the press. But we must remember that the networks are large, multinational corporations. Without endangering press freedom, we must find an answer to this question: Should the networks be the major arbitrators and the most powerful spokesmen on economic, social, technological, and political problems?

Social Uses of Media

A friend of mine who is involved in show business described a certain television commercial in these terms: "This commercial, for whatever reason, for a combination of reasons, had magic in it, pure magic. It translated itself into an awesome power, an overwhelming power."

Magic, awesome power, overwhelming power—was my friend exaggerating? Did his enthusiasm dull his critical sense and carry him away? The commercial that he praised so highly promoted a revival of the musical *Man of La Mancha* in Boston. As he described it, "It's been a good moneymaker, but now we're dealing with a revival, and it's playing in Boston, where it's already appeared four or five times." He estimated that with the backing of the usual professional advertising campaign, the producer could expect to gross about $150,000 a week. The revival had a lot working against it. It was the month of August, the Boston theater where it was to appear was not air-conditioned and its capacity was 4,200, four times the size of the average Broadway house.

The producer promoted the show with one 60-second television commercial that was broadcast many times in Boston and the surrounding area. The commercial was much like many other commercials advertising stage presentations. It consisted of on-the-street interviews with playgoers as they came out of the theater and expressed their enthusiasm for what they had seen. It also included a shot of one of the stars onstage as he sang part of a hit song from the show. Simple in structure, hardly novel in concept, yet somehow it captured the essence of the spirit people attributed to the show. The magic of that commercial cannot

be explained. Its awesome and overwhelming power defy analysis, yet they were such that the production grossed $453,000 in
its first week in Boston. And this was a production that critics
had greeted with lukewarm notices or outright pans. That one
60-second commercial still brings in a profit of 5 to 8 million dollars a year at various box offices throughout the country.

This is an example of the mysterious power of media. But to
what extent have we considered harnessing that power to social
ends? Because they can change attitudes and behavior, media
give us an invaluable opportunity to attack some of the serious
national problems that plague us.

People in various organizations have tried to use the media to
deal with social problems, but their messages usually come to us
in the form of free "public service" advertising. Producers
prepare spot announcements and offer them to stations which
play them in time slots that are difficult to sell to regular advertisers. This free radio and television "public-service" time is generally worthless. Spots directed at children, warning them
against taking rides with strangers, may be broadcast at 2 A.M.,
when only the strangers are watching. Spots that give health information concerning heart attacks may come to us during Saturday morning children's television programs. Stations rarely
broadcast these free, socially oriented commercials at times
when they would reach the audience for which they are intended. The FCC requires networks to reserve time for public-
service messages, but it does not specify particular hours of the
day or times of the year. The stations fulfill their obligations to
"serve the public" in a purely mechanical way: by offering free
time at those odd hours that do not attract commercial advertising. Therefore public-service spots are rarely targeted to the
audience they are supposed to reach.

It is a waste of the awesome power of the media to depend
solely on the charitable impulses of stations or networks. Companies buy time to sell peanut butter, hair tonic, gasoline addi-
tives, chewing gum, and thousands of other products, and use all
the art and science they know to make the media effective. Does
it not make sense for those concerned with social issues, whether
private individuals or public organizations, to buy the media
time to reach the proper audience? People generally assume that

the cost of media time is prohibitive for public-interest organizations, but the value of one targeted commercial broadcast will be far greater than that of ten or fifteen commercials run at haphazard times on stations that do not reach the intended audience. The money spent on the production and distribution of these public-service commercials could pay for a one-shot broadcast at the right time on the right station.

When properly used, the media have a vast behavior-changing potential. This potential lies in two of their important characteristics: First, electronic communication (radio, television, and telephone) is immeasurably faster than other forms: the speed of light. To take this increase in speed for granted is to miss its enormous implications. Consider that a message can now reach anyone in the contiguous United States within one sixty-second of a second.

Second, electronic information allows millions to share and store the same information: the eruption of a volcano, the flooding of a river, the rate of inflation, the number of unemployed, the indictment of a congressman, the death of a national leader, military activity anyplace in the world. People receive these electronic communications everywhere: on the third floor of a skyscraper and on the fifty-third floor; on ranches and in town houses; in suburban mansions and in inner-city slums. People watch and listen to the same programing everywhere. As a result, a large portion of the information we store in our brains is the same as the information stored in everyone else's brain. We can all share a common body of knowledge.

I believe that one of the effects of our being so deeply involved in a world of received media is that we are being turned inward and becoming very receptive to the ways of the East, which have always been inner-directed. Thus we see the growing popularity in the United States of Eastern religions, yoga, various forms of meditation, and Eastern martial arts.

By internalizing the broad knowledge and values disseminated to the whole public through the media, we transform them into our private knowledge and values. The "rugged individualist" of the nineteenth century has become the "common man" of the twentieth century. He is now a resonating cell of the common body. It is this new sense of identity that society can use to affect people's behavior through our new communication technology.

Let us examine an interesting campaign against crime that took place in Japan. In Osaka a dramatic growth in industrialization has spawned a rapid growth in crime. The police utilized an old method of group-oriented societies to attack this problem. They used shame as a tool to control gangster elements, and they directed the campaign not only at the criminals but also at their families, friends, and others who came into daily contact with organized street hoodlums. Because these families and friends were socially embarrassed, they pressured the criminals to change their ways. Osaka's chief of police described this process as "trying to change the waters the gangsters swim in."

In the New York *Times* (May 17, 1977), Andrew H. Malcolm commented on Osaka's approach to reducing crime:

> The strategy, in short, is based on shaming the criminals out of their lawless lives. It is still too early to gauge the program's full effectiveness, but already many gangsters and their families have been isolated socially, a severe punishment in this group-conscious society.

Society's attitude about criminal behavior may be quite different from a criminal's attitude about his own behavior. He may perceive himself as strong, macho, even a hero. When family and friends look upon his behavior with scorn and treat it as shameful, he may find it difficult to maintain his own self-image. Few people manage to survive without support from their social environment.

Anthropologist Edmund Carpenter once described to me what a devastating force shame had been in certain pre-literate cultures:

> You can actually condemn a man to death by shaming him. In oral societies, where the self, the individual, is defined collectively and where he derives his strength from the social structure, when he is denied access to that, cut off from it, he often dies. The secret of this is that they first condemn the man through ridicule, then everyone ignores him. Now, in primitive societies, you often find that there are individuals whose strength of character is strong enough to withstand the condemnation of society. But they generally flee. The result to society is then proof—no man is around who has ever defied the public condemnation. They are either dead or they are gone.

Japan has a more concentrated society than the United States, but we are achieving that closeness through media. Using this principle of shame, the media can penetrate the environment where criminals live and thereby change the waters in which they swim. No one can escape the media. They reach all social environments instantly and continually. We, too, can put principles inherited from early oral cultures to work in our society by making the antisocial person's relationships too uncomfortable for him to endure.

I have an example of a commercial used to shame people into changing their behavior. I designed it for a campaign whose aim was to keep dog owners from allowing their dogs to mess up the sidewalks. Although it deals with behavior that is only mildly criminal, the commercial clearly illustrates the principle of shame. It doesn't just say to the listener, "You must stop your dog from messing up the sidewalks, because it's a bad thing to do." The dog owner probably knows it's a bad thing to do, but he does it anyway. We wanted the dog owner who heard the commercial to feel uncomfortable in relation to other people if he failed to discipline his dog. He will discipline his dog if failure to do so will make him weak and rather dim-witted in the opinion of others. Here is the commercial:

> Let me ask you something. Have you ever seen someone allow his dog to go on the sidewalk? Sometimes right in front of a doorway, maybe your doorway? Did it make you angry? Well, don't get

angry at the poor soul. Feel sorry for him. He's just a person who's not able to train his dog. He's just not capable of it. In fact, after he's had his dog for a short time, what happens? The dog trains him. So the next time you see a person like that on the street, take a good look at him, and while you're looking, feel sorry for him, because you know he just can't help himself, even though he might like to. Some people are strong enough and smart enough to train their dogs to take a few steps off the sidewalk. Other people aren't. Makes you wonder, doesn't it, if the master is at the top of the leash or the bottom of the leash.

We cannot, however, use media to deal with serious crime in such a fashion until we know more about the criminal, his relation to media, and his relation to the people around him. Saturating the air with messages that proclaim that mugging is wrong or that criminals are bad is futile. We have to know the criminal's attitude toward crime, how he gets support for his daily life activity, what he fears most to lose. He may not be afraid of losing his freedom and going to jail, but he might strongly fear the loss of some personal quality (e.g., machismo) that he now attributes to himself. Once research reveals his values, his self-image, his vulnerabilities, we can use media to deprive him of environmental support and thereby affect his behavior.

Many problems in our society have a dollar value, and we can calculate how much a specific problem is costing government, business, or the community at large. A community that can benefit from the solution of serious social problems can bear the expense of a campaign to alleviate them. A continuing problem usually costs more than the solution. For example, in New York City alone people turn in over 245,000 false fire alarms each year. As of this writing, I've been told that the average yearly cost of responding to false fire alarms is more than $170 million.

Can a properly researched media campaign, prepared according to sound communication principles, affect those antisocial elements who turn in false alarms? It is certainly worth a try, since a reduction of even one percent in false alarms could save the city over $1,700,000. I've asked experts in the media field this question: "How much money would the city have to spend on a media campaign to reduce the number of false alarms, and what would be the percentage of the reduction?" The figures they gave me for cost ranged from $50,000 to $2,000,000, and they estimated that spending this money would reduce false alarms by 5 to 50 percent.

The disparity in these figures may appear ridiculous, but if you take the highest cost, $2,000,000, and achieve the lowest percentage of reduction in false alarms, 5 percent, it would still be a paying proposition.

The business community might logically sponsor a campaign designed to reduce the incidence of fires in the home. What is the value to an insurance company of reducing home fires? Paid commercials on home fire protection, run the same day that news broadcasts tell of a particularly tragic fire, would increase people's concern for safety. This can be done by instructing the station to put the commercials on file and run them whenever the news deals with a severe fire. The reduced number of fire claims might save insurance companies more than enough money to cover the cost of this type of targeted commercial. We have, of course, seen home-fire-protection commercials on television, but they have not been time- and task-related in such a manner as to achieve the fullest possible effect.

Similar campaigns can affect the attitude and behavior of both the public and the violators toward shoplifting, graft, energy waste, speeding, mugging, airport thefts, and the like.

One of the most revolting types of crime is attacks on the elderly by young hoodlums. I interviewed a number of policemen on New York City's Senior Citizen Squad, and while they had many ideas for combatting these attacks, they all agreed that their biggest problem was the reluctance of the victims to report the incidents. The policemen felt that they could reduce the number of such attacks by 25 percent if only the elderly would report them.

Ask why the elderly are reluctant to go to the police and most people will answer with an assumption: that it is fear of reprisal, of confronting the hoodlum in court. But when the Senior Citizen Squad delved into this problem they discovered that the elderly held back from reporting crime because of *fear of their own children.* They were afraid that if they reported such attacks, their children would insist that they move to a new and safer neighborhood. But moving is often a deep trauma to the elderly. They are comfortable in their old neighborhoods. They know the landmarks and the shops, and they are close to people with whom they have shared experiences for many years. They find the prospect of moving to a new and strange community more threatening than the existence of street crime where they live.

Media could deal with this situation and involve both the elderly and their children, who often live outside the city. Television and radio spots could give the children of the elderly an understanding of why their parents let crime go unreported. Such commercials could encourage their children to go to their parents and say, "If you're the victim of a crime, please report it, because that will make your neighborhood safer for you, and we know you'd hate to move." Other media, such as print ads, could work toward the same end. Sponsors for such spots could be banks, insurance companies, department stores, city administrations, and other entities whose interests are involved.

Advertising can reach the population at large or any segment of it. People share a fund of information that reaches them through sources they neither control nor pay for: news programs, discussion shows, magazine and newspaper articles, books, word of mouth. Advertising can draw on this commonly shared information and place it in a specific frame of reference. Research can tell us which television shows a target group watches, which radio stations it listens to, and at what time. It can also tell us how a target group reacts to a medium generally, to the subject or program in which we are interested, and to a specific program, magazine, or newspaper. This last type of data is often very important. For example, see how a woman reacted to two commercials that differed in a single but significant respect:

Commercial Number One
You can read about prostitution in a probing series of articles starting Monday in the New York *Post*.

Woman's Reaction
I would just suppose that it would be a sensational, scandalous sort of . . . pseudo-documentary that . . . my guess is that it would be something to exploit prostitution and sell newspapers.

Commercial Number Two

You can read about prostitution in a probing series of articles starting Monday in the New York *Times*.

Same Woman's Reaction

I feel that would be a study, a sociological document . . . something I could rely on as being informative and filled with data.

This experiment reveals one woman's expectations in relation to her experience with and reaction to two newspapers, one a sensational tabloid. Knowledge about these expectations is vital if we are to use media to most deeply affect viewers and listeners.

There are many ways for the government and the general public to use media to solve social problems and achieve social gains, but there have also been many unsuccessful attempts. Joseph A. Califano, Jr., former Secretary of Health, Education, and Welfare, gave us an example of the latter.

During his time as HEW Secretary, Califano was an ardent spokesman against smoking, which he characterized as "slow-motion suicide." He was also on the alert for possible carcinogens in drug products. On May 1, 1979, the New York *Times* carried an AP dispatch that reported, in part, that "Joseph A. Califano . . . said today that the Government would act quickly to remove many well-known nonprescription sleeping aids from the market because of the risk that an ingredient, Methapyrilene, caused cancer."

I certainly favor the curtailing of anything that might cause cancer; yet, when Secretary Califano wanted to bar the sale of certain nonprescription drugs but not the sale of cigarettes, he raised a question that must be answered. Since I suspect that for every case of cancer that Methapyrilene causes, cigarettes cause hundreds, I can only conclude that he treated the tobacco industry with kid gloves for a political reason. We have tobacco states in this country, and these states have congressmen and senators who throw their weight around. We do not have any sleeping-pill states.

When someone asked Jody Powell, President Carter's press secretary, how he reconciled Secretary Califano's anti-smoking campaign with government subsidies to the tobacco industry, Powell replied, "It is not the view of this Administration that we should impose upon the tens of thousands of families whose future would be ruined if we terminated the farm program with regard to tobacco."

The subsidies, however, are not the only contradiction that made the government's position confusing. Secretary Califano suggested "banning cigarettes in most public areas of HEW buildings," and he supported the attempts to ban smoking on commercial airlines. Fine. But if Secretary Califano supported the ban on smoking in planes, why did he not suggest banning the sale of cigarettes in airports? And what about banning the sale and advertising of cigarettes in government buildings, buses, public bus shelters, and Amtrak trains?

Califano was quite vocal about the hazards of smoking, but by doing nothing more assertive than asking people not to smoke in selected (and limited) public facilities, the Secretary communicated that smoking is more a nuisance to others than a health menace.

I cite these contradictions to illustrate a way of thinking and behaving that characterizes public agencies. The same thinking characterizes their approach to media. Under Califano, a division of HEW asked me to answer an ad calling for bids on an anti-smoking media campaign. The ad asked those who submitted bids for evidence that they had "knowledge and experience in producing outstanding national advertising campaigns in all media in such product fields as automobiles, beverages, and food products." This indicates that HEW was planning to "sell" non-smoking like a product, rather than recognizing that the smoking problem demands a deep psychological understanding of why people smoke.

I was also shocked to learn that HEW wanted much of the anti-smoking campaign to be treated as a public service, and Califano suggested that the networks make available public-service time for anti-smoking messages. The public-service approach might have an impact on insomniacs (the networks provide a lot of public service at 2 A.M.) but not on the general population. Was it too much to hope that HEW would put into its anti-smoking campaign a fraction of the amount of money that the government pours into subsidies for the tobacco industry? Other government agencies function differently. The Army buys advertising space and time for its recruiting drives. The

Post Office buys advertising space and time to sell stamps. But the anti-smoking campaign had no budget for media and planned to beg the networks and stations for a handout.

The same government that claims to be interested in helping people break the smoking habit is offering cigarettes *at the lowest possible price* at the PXs on U. S. Army posts. The government's *behavior* in subsidizing tobacco and promoting its distribution is a *message*, just as a media campaign is a message. If the two signals are contradictory and the public is exposed to both, how can the government possibly influence people to stop smoking?

The government's media efforts against smoking have been hopelessly outclassed by the tobacco advertisers. Let's look at an ad that appeared in the November 13, 1978, issue of *Time* magazine. Inside the front cover Philip Morris, Inc., had a six-page gatefold ad for its Marlboro cigarettes. It was a gorgeous ad, almost totally visual and quite breathtaking. It was not aimed to deceive. It made no product claims whatever. It was designed for effect, and the effect was powerful. Here, except for two lines identifying various Marlboro cigarettes, was the entire print message:

> This is a special place where some do what others only dream about. And life has a flavor all its own. . . . Come to where the flavor is. . . . Come to Marlboro Country. . . . Wherever men smoke for flavor, that's Marlboro Country.

That's all the copy there was in that six-page ad, but we hardly bothered to read it, because we were so affected by the background of sweeping plains, majestic hills, and snow-capped mountains, rugged cowboys roping cattle, wandering herds, a chuck wagon and campfire at night. A dream of paradise. The copy, of course, said very little. The visuals, exquisite, eye-filling, said a great deal.

This ad followed every rule and regulation that the FTC instituted to govern cigarette advertising. It contained the prescribed Surgeon General's statement, which was in no way hidden or disguised. It stood out, black printing in a white box, against a background of color. No one could miss it. It was the government's counter ad within the cigarette ad.

Remember the old saying "You can take the boy out of the farm, but you can't take the farm out of the boy"? Well, you can take cigarette ads out of television, but you can't take television out of cigarette ads. The Marlboro ad was ingeniously designed to appeal to those sensitivities that television commercials have developed. The ad evoked a sensuous response: the wide-open spaces, fresh sparkling air, fleecy clouds, fragrant breezes blowing over verdant plains, hearty men sharing food and a fire under the stars. It associated smoking with an environment that was beautiful, exciting—and even healthful! Its message was that Marlboro cigarettes are an integral part of life in that clean, invigorating environment.

Tracy Westen, of the FTC, has referred to this type of ad as "nonverbal deception," but there was nothing illegal in it. Marlboro didn't say, "Smoking is good for you." Marlboro just showed us America the Beautiful and included smoking in that vision.

The Marlboro ad was a masterpiece which proved that cigarette advertisers can obey every restriction in the book and still sell cigarettes. Fully one third of the printed matter in that ad consisted of the Surgeon General's warning and the tar and nicotine ratings. Clearly, the more compelling message was conveyed nonverbally. If the inclusion of the Surgeon General's warning in cigarette advertising actually *hurt* the sale of cigarettes, the cigarette companies would cease to advertise.

My point here is that HEW has something to learn from the Marlboro folks and should develop powerful and prominent antismoking ads that try to control the environmental stimuli to which people bring their own reactions.

I once designed a series of anti-smoking commercials for the American Cancer Society. In a number of them I tried to evoke a feeling common to all parents: concern for their children. In one of the television commercials, the audience saw two little children, a boy and a girl, playing in an attic. They were dressing up in their parents' old wedding clothes. As we watched them in this familiar bit of children's play, we heard the voice of the announcer saying, "Children love to imitate their parents. . . . Children learn by imitating their parents. . . . Do you smoke cigarettes?" The commercial concluded with the visual symbol of the American Cancer Society.

Here is a radio commercial designed to evoke the same response:

Announcer
Ever see a four-year-old drive a car?
Four-year-old Boy
When I'm going somewheres sometime I go in the car and I drive the steering wheel and honk the horn just like Daddy.
Announcer
Kids imitate their parents . . . the good and the bad.
Four-year-old Boy
Look, Mom, I'm smoking a cigarette! Looks just like Daddy, doesn't it?
Announcer
Looks like a cigarette, just like Daddy. . . . Do you smoke— Daddy?

Electronic media are tunable, by which I mean they may be transmitted broadly or narrowly, more or less frequently, and with greater or lesser intensity. They can be direct or tangential. We can control all these factors. For this reason a rock group isn't concerned about the acoustical environment in which it performs. The rock group simply tunes the hall by turning a little knob on its amplifiers to fit the environment.

We can tune the electronic media in this manner, but first we have to learn to observe the effects of these media and determine what causes these effects. Then we can isolate the elements that produce these effects and use them to our advantage. An extreme but quite interesting example of this is Buckminster Fuller's idea for increasing the interest of the Indian people in science. He suggested sending them portable radios. Radios would have the effect of increasing literacy, and an increase in literacy would have the effect of encouraging the study of science. If people with serious problems are literate, they will try to read whatever can help them solve those problems.

Terrorists have learned to tune the media. They monitor the news programs and schedule their terrorist acts in such a way as to tune the news coverage for their purposes. In fact, they often take over the news programs and dictate their content. They may send tapes to a television station, as in the case of the Patty Hearst kidnapping, or they may call upon television personalities to act as their intermediaries. Chris Borgen, of WCBS-TV, was used in this capacity, and former Yippie Abbie Hoffman turned his arrest for selling cocaine into a media event by "surrendering" to Barbara Walters. (We saw earlier instances of this when criminals turned themselves in to Walter Winchell.) Since there are often lives at stake in these situations, terrorists and criminals can blackmail stations into compliance. The stations may intellectually resent being used in this fashion, but they find the listener involvement very profitable.

People are much concerned with criticizing the media, demanding program changes, the curtailment of commercials, an end to advertising products designed for small children, a moratorium on television violence. But it is more important to learn how to use the power of media than it is to attempt to curtail that power, to use media not to achieve trivial ends but in the cause of those social and political struggles that involve ordinary people: the fight to save a school, change a zoning law, halt the construction of an atomic power plant (or speed its construction if that is the position you take), protest the lack of police protection, demand an end to a war, work for the repeal of blue laws, prevent condemnation of certain buildings, ensure better garbage collection, diminish shoplifting, or cut down on street crime.

The conventional means of conducting such campaigns have usually involved mass protests or demonstrations, yet such protests and demonstrations are becoming obsolete. Their effectiveness today cannot compare with the results that a sophisticated use of media would achieve.

Following the breakdown of the nuclear plant at Three Mile Island, in Pennsylvania, the nation experienced an upsurge of protest against the growing national dependence on nuclear energy. The high point of the protests was a rally in Washington which drew between 75,000 and 100,000 people. I once asked the leader of a public-interest group how much money, on the average, a person had to spend to attend a rally in Washington.

He made a cautious estimate of 40 dollars to cover the cost of food, travel, and lodging. If we accept the lower figure, of 75,000, who attended this anti-nuclear protest, the people who participated spent a total of at least $3 million. With that $3 million the anti-nuclear organizations could have bought commercial time to get into every home in the country, say exactly what they wanted to say, and say it free of editorial cuts or comments by newscasters.

Television and radio report mass rallies on regular programing time—news, interviews, panel discussion shows. But in the non-commercial broadcast time the networks can frame the participants in a rally to fit their own prejudices. They photograph rallies mainly to catch "dramatic" moments, even if those moments may be atypical of the general character of the rally. If they choose, they can present participants as belonging to a lunatic fringe, as loud and obstreperous, or even as objects of scorn.

When a public-interest group pays for its own media, it can present itself on its own terms and in the best possible light. Just as groups can get the best speakers to speak at a rally, they can get knowledgeable people to prepare their commercials. In many cases such people will volunteer their time, but even if they ask for a fee, remember that the restaurants that feed demonstrators and the bus companies that carry them to their destination also charge fees.

In a small city, a two- or three-thousand-dollar media investment can have far greater effect than almost any mass rally. (I say "almost any" because there have been mass rallies in which the psychological effect of a mass turnout has tremendous importance. Such was the case with Martin Luther King's march on Washington.)

Some time ago I met with a group of students from the City University of New York (CUNY). The group had organized an ongoing protest against an increase in tuition at the school. They held many rallies outside City Hall or the Board of Higher Education. After each rally, every participant was out of pocket a few dollars for transportation, coffee, and the like.

I spoke to Ellen Straus, of radio station WMCA, and she

agreed to give the students an hour's time on her radio station. I asked the students to buy time to advertise the radio program, put up posters around the schools, and alert their parents and friends to listen to WMCA at the appointed hour. During the program, the students could remain in their classrooms while this "electronic rally" reached everyone in the City University, the mayor, the Board of Higher Education, and people throughout the metropolitan area. In addition, I suggested that the program be constructed so that students could call in questions. Speakers could also take pledges of contributions to finance further actions.

The students, however, did not respond to this plan. Apparently the social aspects of the rally were more important to them than its effectiveness. They had a sentimental attachment to the atmosphere of camaraderie and fraternity that surrounds such rallies. They did not understand that in this era the largest and most powerful political and social force is television and radio. Because of this lack of understanding, the "electronic rally" is a tool that has not yet been used or seriously considered, except for telethons and some religious programs.

Ironically, the news coverage of the student rallies presented them in a way that only made the students appear disruptive. The effect of the media coverage, coverage which they did not control, was negative. The tuition went up.

The reluctance these students showed toward replacing a live demonstration with a media campaign is not unusual. Joe Napolitan, who managed Hubert Humphrey's media campaign in the 1968 presidential race, reports that Humphrey often passed up the opportunity to appear on local television (and reach a few hundred thousand people) in favor of meeting forty or fifty people in a shopping center. Humphrey probably felt more comfortable pressing the flesh and talking to such groups than he did before a camera, a microphone, and an invisible audience. Yet political analysts such as Joe Napolitan believe that Humphrey's failure to fully utilize the media may have led to his defeat.

The modern media citizen, however, is slowly emerging. Consider Jack Nelen, of Springfield, Massachusetts. Mr. Nelen's family owned a furniture store in that city for one hundred years. The local school district wanted to condemn the property and use it to build a new state technical high school. Understandably, Jack Nelen opposed this.

Mr. Nelen's brother-in-law, a professional media researcher, took a poll of Springfield citizens and discovered that 68 percent of the community opposed using Mr. Nelen's property as the site for the new school, because it was situated in a rundown and decaying area. The public wanted the school built on the hills overlooking Springfield.

Mr. Nelen then formed a committee called Citizens Opposed to State Tech, a misnomer because they were not opposed to the building of the school but only to the site on which the school board intended to build it. He personally funded research and publicity and hired me to design a media campaign. His total budget was fifteen thousand dollars.

We did a few radio commercials and one television commercial, based on a remark someone once made to me to the effect that he had never heard of any group of people who consciously voted for a tax increase. The copy on the radio and television spots was quite similar. In the television spot the screen showed only the word TAXES. At first this word was only partly visible at the bottom of the screen. Then, as the announcer read the copy, the word TAXES kept appearing on the screen. Images of the word piled up on one another. Finally, a montage of the word TAXES in many colors filled the entire screen. The effect was that of taxes piling upon taxes. The copy read:

> There's a lot of confusion about the new school the mayor and some other politicians want to build on the corner of State Street and Walnut Street. No matter how much the state contributes, the school complex will cost more than 44 million dollars, straight out of the taxpayer's pocket. Even using the mayor's own figures, by his own admission the city would have to pay about a million dollars a year in carrying charges alone. Think of what that will mean to your tax rate. That's why we urge you to vote "no" on November 30. . . . Paid for by Citizens Opposed to State Tech.

November 30 was the date set for a vote on this one issue.

Consider the background of this campaign. The incumbent mayor and the three mayors who had preceded him all favored condemnation of Jack Nelen's store. In addition, the Board of Education, the City Council, and all the city's newspapers and

radio and television stations supported the condemnation proposal. The Sunday before the election, Springfield's ministers de-
livered sermons supporting the proposal.

Our opponents launched their own campaign and spent about
eight dollars to our one. Yet all their media were working in our
favor, because every message they broadcast assured the people
of Springfield that their taxes would not go up quite as high as
we claimed they would. They would only go up by so much. But
the people of Springfield didn't want their taxes to go up at all.

The election results came in, and a whopping 67 percent of
the voters turned down the condemnation proposal.

In another campaign, I was interested in defeating a bill in
the New York State legislature. This bill would have banned
Sunday shopping for some items and allowed it for others. To
my mind it seemed like a very capricious piece of legislation. Be-
sides, like many others, I enjoy Sunday shopping.

I called people I knew at the Bamberger chain of department
stores, in New Jersey, to ask which New York retailers might be
interested in working with me to defeat this bill, and they
suggested that I get in touch with Macy's, a sister company store.
Macy executives agreed to pay a polling organization to find out
how the general population felt about Sunday shopping. Then we
bought time for two radio commercials, one planned for broadcast
in Albany and New York City, the other in Albany alone. Here
is the commercial designed for both cities:

Did you ever do something and then say to yourself, "Did I really
do that?" Well, you and I personally elected every single member
of the New York State legislature. But do you know what they're
planning to do to us in two or three days? They're planning to pass
laws to close department stores and supermarkets and cut off our
Sunday shopping. The blue laws were first passed in 1781, when
people were crossing the country in covered wagons and Napoleon
was just becoming a teenager. So we were wondering, wouldn't our
legislators like to get on their horses and join us in the twentieth
century? Maybe what they need is encouragement, so call them at
(212) 488-3848. Just leave the message that you like to shop on
Sunday and want the freedom to do it every Sunday right up to
Election Day. . . . Paid for by the New York State Retailers Coalition to Continue Sunday Shopping. . . . (212) 488-3848.

A soft-spoken woman with a bedroom voice recorded the second commercial, designed for the Albany area:

Do you know what Stanley says? He says we can't buy a sofa on Sunday. Stanley says it's all right if we want to buy a sailboat, but the crib and the baby carriage? Out! Can't buy them. You know what else Stanley says? He says we can buy an antique chair. We need a kitchen chair, but Stanley says we can't buy that. You don't know who Stanley is? Stanley Steingut, the New York State Assembly Speaker. He's backing a law that will close the department stores and supermarkets on Sunday. Stanley wants the blue laws back again. You want to call Stanley? I'll give you his number: (518) 742-3100. I'm glad you're calling. If Stanley knows how you feel about it, maybe he'll change his mind. . . . Paid for by the New York State Retailers Coalition to Continue Sunday Shopping. . . . Tell Stanley how you feel. . . . (518) 742-3100.

The day after the first broadcast of this commercial, Stanley Steingut had to change his office number. A few days later the legislature defeated the proposed ban on Sunday shopping.

During the summer of 1980, shortly before the Democratic National Convention was to meet in New York City, New York's Coalition of Uniformed Services scheduled negotiations for a new contract for the city police. The Coalition of Uniformed Services did not want a strike. They wanted a settlement. The police had already made many important concessions to a city in deep financial trouble, but inflation, the high cost of living, and the level of their salaries made it imperative for them to get relief.

I had done work for Phil Caruso in his campaign for the presidency of the Patrolmen's Benevolent Association, the post he now holds. I had also worked with Ken McFeeley, the former president of the PBA. Both of them assured me that they sincerely hoped that the police would not have to strike. But it appeared that the city administration wanted a strike, and because that was so, the negotiations were getting nowhere. Because they are municipal workers, the city could levy fines against striking policemen under the terms of the Taylor Law, and those fines could pay the cost of any wage increase the police might win.

It was my opinion that we could use media to prevent a strike, but to do this we would have to involve Mayor Ed Koch. Traditionally, the mayor does not participate in negotiations of this sort. He waits for a settlement and then comes in to announce the terms and sign the contract. But if a strike was to be averted, we had to bring the mayor into the negotiations immediately.

Here is one of the three commercials we ran:

Mayor Koch, remember the great job the city policemen did during the transit strike, when our city was in deep financial trouble and the banks refused to buy our bonds? Remember how the uniformed officers bought those bonds with their pension-fund money? Remember the one hundred uniformed officers who died in the last five years in performance of their duties? Mayor Koch, over the last five years workers in outside industry received an average wage increase of 50 percent. The uniformed services got only 8 percent. We understood that the city was in trouble, and we bit the bullet. But we just can't do it any more. Most of us have to take a second job. Our wives have to work so we can make ends meet. We're the people the city calls on when it's in trouble. Now we're calling on you because we're in trouble. We get the impression you want us to strike, and we don't deserve that treatment. If we're wrong, prove it by putting a decent and reasonable proposal on the negotiating table. . . . Paid for by the Coalition of Uniformed Services.

President Phil Caruso, of the PBA, told of the effect of this commercial. He said, "The immediate reaction when it hit the air was that we got signals from the mayor's office that they wanted those commercials removed as quickly as possible, and they wanted to sit down and talk about a settlement. So it paid dividends immediately."

Shortly after we ran the commercial, Chuck Scarborough said on an NBC News broadcast, "Earlier today the negotiators got a surprise visit. We have more from Jim Ryan." And Jim Ryan reported, "Union leaders were late arriving at the talks this morning. Five minutes later they got that surprise visitor, the man who vowed to remain apart from the talks, Mayor Koch. After spending about ten minutes with the negotiators, and leaving to a round of applause, the mayor told reporters the reasons for his visit." NBC then showed a videotape of the mayor saying, "I came here to express my appreciation to the uniformed services for their heroic work and for the sacrifices they have made since the fiscal crisis."

The negotiations proceeded to a satisfactory settlement. The police did not have to strike.

Late last year a friend introduced me to Stanley G. Jones, vice-president of development for the United Design & Engineering Corporation, of St. Louis, Missouri. Mr. Jones was disturbed because although on a number of occasions his firm had submitted the low bid for public construction funded by Washington, it had not been awarded the contract. The most recent example of this had taken place in Illinois's 24th Congressional District. (The United Design & Engineering Corporation, of Missouri, did considerable work in Illinois, just across the Mississippi.)

To meet this situation we prepared two commercials, one for Washington, D.C., and the other for the 24th Congressional District in Illinois. Here is the one designed for Illinois:

> Congressman Paul Simon, what do you think of spending $175,917 of government money and getting absolutely nothing in return? Well, that's exactly what's happening in the 24th Congressional District. Recently Pope, Salina, and Menard counties asked for bids on the construction of low-rent public housing, to be funded by the Department of Housing and Urban Development. But you know what? The contracts were not awarded to the lowest bidders. Instead they went to firms who bid more than $175,000 above the lowest bids. Why? We can't find out. Maybe you could ask Mr. Herman Atkerson, Mr. Howard Atkerson, Mr. Alfred Mason, the chairmen of those counties, whether it's their practice to spend more than they have to for public construction projects. This question is asked by Concerned Taxpayers of Illinois's 24th Congressional District. Aren't you suspicious, Congressman Simon? Would you spend your money that way?

The commercial used in the Washington area was fundamentally the same, but it omitted the names of the local county chairmen. Only the future can tell the effect of these commercials, but I am convinced that low bidders on public construction in the 24th Congressional District now have a much better chance of having their bids accepted.

Another commercial I designed helped force a revision of the Massachusetts State budget:

> You know the expression, pulling the wool over somebody's eyes? Well, I was just looking at the state's new budget, that two-and-a-

half-billion-dollar budget, and in between things like the State Police and hospitals for the chronically ill and other things we need, at four or five state institutions there were budgets for herdsmen, poultrymen, dairymen, swineherdsmen, and even an assistant herdsman. But only one of these institutions has any animals. I'm sorry, but it's true. And you got to ask yourself, who's pulling the wool over whose eyes? I mean, that state budget is in the legislature and somebody should take a closer look at two and a half billion dollars of your money and mine, just to see how it is being spent. That's why this is paid for by Citizens for Economy in Government. . . . Herdsmen, poultrymen, dairymen, swineherdsmen.

I have shown how a small store protected its interests against a whole city bureaucracy, how larger stores successfully mobilized public support for Sunday shopping, how the police in New York City averted a strike and won a negotiated contract, how we tried to correct inequities in the funding of public projects, and how citizens used media to bring about changes in a state budget. These are relatively restricted, special interests. But the modern media citizen who is interested in national issues such as the campaign to pass the ERA or to defend the right of abortion must inevitably learn that media are his or her most powerful weapon. In addition to selling detergents, the media can be a great ally to those who seek to solve social problems.

Work and Time

Automation is often presented as a means of replacing manual work in modern society. True, automation does more and more of the work that men and women used to do, but the media have also replaced work in ways we may be aware of, and in the future they will do so in new ways that we have not yet conceived.

It's my belief that in the health field alone the media save the nation millions of doctor-patient hours daily. We no longer go to the doctor for treatment of minor ailments such as headaches, muscle aches, sore throat, false teeth that refuse to stay put, athlete's foot, dysmenhorrhea, itching scalp. The list is endless. Today few seek professional advice for such conditions unless they are alarmingly severe, and so, without even having to make an appointment, we accept the media as our doctor for minor complaints. The media pay house calls. We feel free to take the advice of commercials that tell us what to do for these minor ailments because we know that the FTC and other government agencies monitor these ads for false or misleading information.

Media can also play a role in preventive medicine involving more serious conditions. Dr. Frank Field, science reporter and meteorologist for NBC-TV news, introduced women in his audience to the process of self-examination for breast cancer. Because we could see a woman correctly examine herself for breast lumps, we absorbed the process with an accuracy that words alone could never have supplied.

On another news broadcast, Dr. Field introduced the audience to the Heimlich Maneuver, a simple process by which one can force a choking person to dislodge whatever is caught in his throat. This program and many repeat telecasts have already saved many lives.

Both of these segments taught thousands of people to perform processes that they would have had to be taught individually before the advent of electronic media.

With discussion shows, the media again bypass the reading process and personal visits to the doctor, to spread medical information and knowledge. Such programs go far beyond easy "home remedy" medicine. A television or radio discussion on a medical problem will usually feature top medical specialists in the field, who can give advice and information to millions of the less affluent who cannot afford or don't have access to a personal physician.

Even the medical shows such as "General Hospital," "The Doctors," and "Emergency," which are carefully researched to ensure medical accuracy, have an important effect in making people more familiar with and aware of the hospital setting. Many viewers have never seen the inside of a real hospital, and such programs help by removing fear of the unknown.

In August of 1978 New York City suffered an outbreak of that form of pneumonia called Legionnaire's disease. Investigators traced the source of the infection to New York's garment district. Workers in that district were jittery. Radio and television, acting responsibly, called on medical experts to acquaint the people of New York with the symptoms of the disease. News programs told them when it would be necessary to seek medical aid, assured them that help was readily available, and warned against exaggerating the severity of the problem, which was not of epidemic proportions.

Commercials have also been used in campaigns against venereal disease and to encourage parents to see to it that their children get measles shots and other immunizations. In the past, such "work" would have been accomplished exclusively by individual word of mouth, doctors speaking to patients, pamphlets, or volunteer workers going from door to door or setting up booths on street corners.

The media have taken over the major portion of the work involved in political campaigning: the printing of leaflets, posters, and brochures, and their distribution by mail or hand. Such distribution still continues but on a much smaller scale. Years ago, at election time, fifteen or twenty political canvassers would ring my doorbell. For the past five years not one single political canvasser has disturbed my peace. The work involved in a candidate's travel has also been cut to a minimum. During election campaigns the candidate travels primarily via media. In Washington, Congressman Ike Skelton has cut down on his visits to Missouri by using the conference phone as a means of returning to his community anytime he pleases. He uses this conference phone to talk to groups of his constituents. Far from causing him to be perceived as an absentee representative, his phone conferences bring him much closer to his constituents.

Discussion shows and political commercials have drastically reduced the need for personal appearances by the candidates. In the fall of 1980, I worked on six campaigns, each of which had one central office but no local offices. Candidates' staffs have become smaller and more centralized. Televised debates save travel time for both the candidates and the public. People keep track of political campaign activities by sitting in front of their sets.

The media have also reset the clocks. In 1878, Sandford Fleming, a Canadian Scot, devised our current system of time zones. He proposed that we adopt for the earth twenty-four standard meridians 15 degrees apart in longitude, starting from Greenwich, England, and use these to divide the day into twenty-four time zones. Since then we have kept track of time by using these time zones. Since different parts of our globe always stand in different relationship to the sun, these zones were a convenience for living, a way of ensuring that whenever the sun stood at its zenith it was twelve noon.

Electricity has seriously weakened this concept of time. Like
the international airlines, which operate on Greenwich mean
time no matter what their location, we are beginning to operate
on a universal time scheme, because the meaning of time zones
changes when people communicate across them.

Before electricity, man had a different sense of the relationship between time and space. People couldn't speak to one
another across different time zones unless they lived at the bor-
der of a zone. Today the telephone, radio, and television have
made such communication commonplace. More crucial, the separation of geographic areas into time zones is no longer a reliable indicator of how people relate to each other in terms of
time. As the telephone company says, long distance is the next-
best thing to being there. The people of the world in all its time
zones can share events as they are happening now: the eruption
of a volcano, the visit of a Pope, the funeral of a world leader,
the breaking of a sports record. The reading on their local clocks
is irrelevant. This phenomenon is so familiar that people have
not paused to assess its great significance. We accept it as being
in the natural order of things without realizing that it has
reversed the natural order of things. When we communicated
over long distances primarily by mail, we were never confronted
wih the time differences in the various zones. Today we find that
many digital watches can show the time in several time zones,
and some clocks show the time, A.M. and P.M., in all the time
zones.

Today we can watch and listen to a round-table discussion on
Arab oil economics in which the participants speak from four
separate locations: New York, California, Japan, and Egypt.
They are talking to one another from different time zones, and
yet what they are saying is happening now. Similarly, we can
watch a presidential press conference now, regardless of the
time zone we are living in. In the last presidential election, President Carter was severely criticized for making his concession
speech many hours before the polls closed on the West Coast.
As a consequence, a good number of voters who would otherwise have turned out to cast their ballots remained home instead.
It is even believed that some West Coast candidates might have

been winners instead of losers had not the President conceded so early.

Early wireless brought this breakdown of time to the front pages of newspapers. A wireless message from Japan could result in a newspaper story that told of an event that would be happening tomorrow (our time) but that had already happened in Japan (their time). People today are confronted as never before with these confusions of time. You call someone in California at two in the afternoon and he answers the phone by saying, "Good morning."

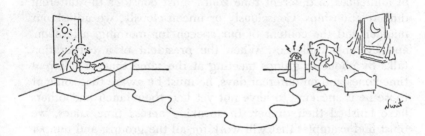

The function of time in business has also changed. The length of time required for a letter to travel from New York to Chicago, or for a salesman to drive from one city to another, no longer establishes fixed limits around which executives pattern other aspects of business. The time lag between sending a message and receiving an answer, so important in an exchange of letters, does not exist when we speak directly on the telephone. People write fewer letters than they used to, and this causes a vicious circle: Because the letters are fewer, post-office income drops, the Postal Service makes fewer pickups and deliveries, and because the services are reduced, people rely still more heavily on the phone.

Business presentations today often restructure time by placing events recorded on film or tape in the context of current events. We can speed up the history of a company to reveal a pattern, or we may take a single event and slow it down to reveal its structure, because we are now able to manipulate time in the same way an artist makes a mosaic. Sears, Roebuck speeded up history when it offered a two-minute presentation that showed the products advertised in their first catalog, printed over one hundred years ago. The presentation demonstrated the variety of products and how they have changed over the years. Companies engaged in the new system of tearing down buildings by blasting, a form of instant demolition, have slowed down history by viewing films of the process in slow motion in order to perfect the technique for future use.

We have entered this new relation to time without being aware of how it has affected our thinking or the implications it holds for other areas of business. A business presentation aimed at audiences in different time zones must consider the different time relationships. Consciously or unconsciously, we adjust our manner and the content of our speech for morning, afternoon, and evening audiences. When the president of a corporation talks by phone to groups meeting at the same time in different time zones and on different days, he must be aware that some of those he is speaking to have not yet had their lunch and others have finished their dinner. In speaking across time zones, we must find examples that will work for all the groups, and temper our manner of speaking for each time relationship. We cannot say simple things like "good morning" or "good evening." We cannot even suggest that certain things be done immediately, because for some the day is already coming to a close, while for others it may be just beginning.

Electronic media have reset our clocks to read *now*.

The Microphone
and the Church

New York magazine quoted Frank Sinatra as saying, "The microphone is the singer's basic instrument, not the voice. You have to learn to play it like it was a saxophone."

Nowadays a live performer, using a microphone, can make each listener, sitting in the privacy of his bedroom, living room, or auto, feel as though the song is meant expressly for him; with an adjustment of the volume control on the amplifying system, the same singer can reach the last row of any concert hall or perform for eighty thousand people gathered on the Central Park Mall.

The microphone has also brought about more-subtle and unexpected changes. It could be said that the microphone, not a Vatican council, changed the liturgy of the Catholic Church. The architecture of all large cathedrals features hard surfaces, walls of stone or marble, stone ceilings, tiled or stone floors. The voices of priests and bishops who spoke in such surroundings were given an awesome quality. Echoes confused every sound, adding to the mystery of the architectural environment and the religious experience.

Before the churches installed microphones, the Catholic priest conducted most of the service with his back to his parishioners, and he intoned the liturgy in Latin. In any ordinary auditory atmosphere, the dimly heard Latin sounded like little more than a murmur, but in the spacious, highly reverberant reaches of the church it created a tonality and wonder appropriate to meditation.

Then came the microphone, with its ability to make the voice of the priest clearly audible to everyone. The Latin words were

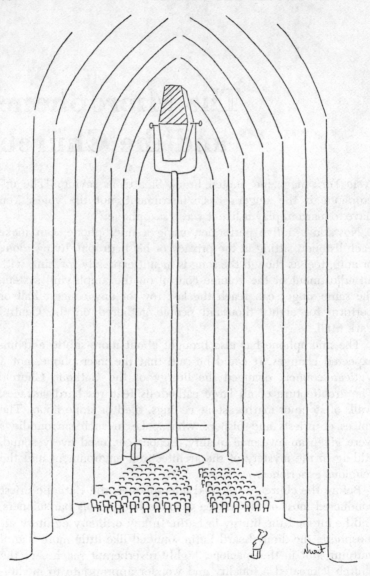

no longer an indistinguishable chant, or what McLuhan called "the blessed mutter." Parishioners now heard the words, even though they were Latin words. When people constantly hear a language, it is inevitable that they should want to understand it.

Thus began the move to translate the liturgy into the native languages of Catholic parishioners throughout the world. The microphone turned the priest around, so that he now faces the congregation.

The first religious broadcast in the United States took place on January 2, 1921, when Pittsburgh's radio station KDKA broadcast the vesper services from the Calvary Episcopalian Church. As the years went by, religious broadcasts became commonplace. Like the trumpets that blew down the walls of Jericho, radio and television helped crumble the walls of the churches. When religious leaders first took to broadcasting services over radio, they were concerned that the collection plate would pass by those who gave up church attendance and stayed at home to listen. This fear carried over into television, and when the Catholic Church first permitted the televising of services at Christmas, Easter, and other holidays, we often saw this printed disclaimer on the bottom of the screen: "Watching this show in no way substitutes for attendance in church."

But it didn't take long for other churches to realize that the radio and television audience would increase, rather than decrease, church revenue. Today toll-free numbers now serve numerous church groups whose fund-raising ability is quite staggering. It is not unusual for a church group to raise millions of dollars in a matter of months.

No longer are the faithful to be found exclusively in church on Sunday. The church is everywhere and anywhere it finds an audience of followers. On Sundays in Poland the Catholic churches are usually filled, but on Sunday, October 22, 1978, they were all but empty, because that was the day of the investiture of John Paul II, the first Polish Pope. The Polish people wanted to see the ceremony of investiture on television. They didn't abandon the church. They simply found church elsewhere.

Radio and television created ecclesiastical "stars," the first of whom was Father Charles Coughlin, the "Radio Priest." Others followed quickly, notably Bishop Fulton J. Sheen, Billy Graham, Oral Roberts, and Dr. Norman Vincent Peale. Rabbi Stephen S. Wise was a Jewish ecclesiastical "star."

Black churches on radio and television have affected another area of our culture. These broadcasts have familiarized a whole generation of young people, black and white, with black gospel and folk music. The media secularized this music and gave it a national character.

In matters of faith, the primary change that the media have brought about is the democratization of religion. Everyone can listen, observe, and compare the rituals and mode of observance of many religions. Whereas a Catholic may once have felt ill at ease attending a Baptist church, or a Jew similarly uncomfortable sitting in on Catholic services, people today feel less self-conscious about watching the services of other churches on

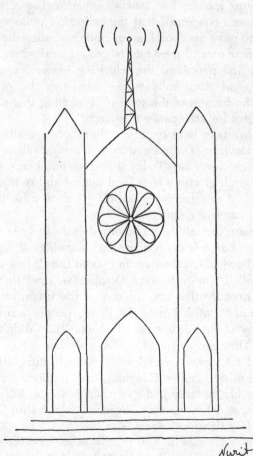

television. The dimensions of many religions are suddenly available to us if we wish to explore them.

Any religious leader today who uses radio and television has access to the minds of millions. An example of this phenomenon is the Moral Majority, a coalition of fundamentalist evangelists who now wield immense social and political power. An estimate of their strength and their understanding of media can be gleaned from a pamphlet published by Convocation, a joint convention of the National Association of Evangelists and National Religious Broadcasters, held January 25–28, 1981, in Washington, D.C. This was a gathering of religious leaders all of whom believe in an absolutely literal interpretation of the Bible. They consider any religion other than fundamentalist Christianity to be idolatry.

If their approach to theology is primitive, their approach to media certainly is not. In their pamphlet, Convocation claimed to have brought together leaders from some thirty thousand churches and fourteen hundred religious radio and television stations. They also claim that one new religious radio station goes on the air every week and one new religious television station goes on the air every month. Bear in mind that to the Moral Majority, "religious" is synonymous with believing in fundamentalist evangelism.

Convocation set up workshops that were all devoted to improving and expanding Moral Majority broadcasting. Workshops were offered in such subjects as:

> Research
> Management
> Programing
> Sales
> Basics of Broadcasting
> Audience Research
> Satellites, Cables, and Earth Stations
> Time Management
> FCC Trends
> Reaching Europe and the U.S.S.R.
> Africa and the Middle East
> Open Doors of Asia
> New Technology and Trends

Time Buying
Fund Raising
Producing and Marketing a Program
Advanced Video Technique.

As of today these groups are buying more radio and television time than very many of our largest national advertisers combined. They also own or are purchasing many radio and television stations. In addition to their evangelical media efforts, they are using media to wage political warfare against any politician, in office or running for office, who differs with their political and moral viewpoints.

The Moral Majority was founded in 1979 by the Reverend Jerry Falwell, and today as many people know his name as know the name of any Catholic, Protestant, or Jewish religious leader. Falwell began modestly by broadcasting his "Old Time Gospel Hour" as a local radio and television show in Lynchburg, Virginia. Today his program is on 324 stations in the United States, Canada, and the Caribbean, and he reaches an estimated audience of 50 million viewers. He operates on an annual budget of 56 million tax-free dollars, and his Moral Majority has captured the Republican Party apparatus in Alaska.

No one can question the propriety of the media activities of the Moral Majority. The Moral Majority is exercising its right, under the Constitution, to be heard, and that right must be respected. But what we must also face is the possible consequence of so much media power in the hands of a group that is determined to affect moral, ethical, and political standards for the rest of the country. The original alliance between religion and radio may turn out to be one of the most powerful in history, an alliance between the first and the second gods.

Political Communication

From its very inception, radio, with its ability to get inside the minds of its listeners, began to undermine the strength of political parties in the United States. Television accelerated the process. The media have replaced political parties as the main channel of communication to the electorate and the vehicle for organizing people and getting them out to the polls. Millions upon millions of Americans belong to no political party and feel the need for none. They vote for candidates without regard to the party label attached to them. As a consequence, more and more voters consider themselves political independents, and the split ticket is a common phenomenon. The media, rather than a political party or club, now inform and form our political views and behavior.

Before the media brought politics into the home, someone interested in the political process could not hear and see candidates or engage in political activity without leaving his hearth. If he wanted to hear a political speaker he went to a rally. His friends and neighbors could observe him going there and make note of whether he favored the Democratic or the Republican Party. He might even attend a Socialist Party meeting and run the risk of being fired by his employer and ostracized by his fellow workers and his local political-party structure. This party structure could also monitor his behavior by noting whether he walked out on a candidate during a speech or failed to applaud along with the faithful. The party in power dispensed government jobs, and anyone who owed his employment to one party would think twice before going to a rival-party rally.

Radio brought privacy to political communication. A citizen could now listen in his home to any candidate on any station and no one would know. He could even use earphones if he was so inclined.

Previously, most women could not participate in the political process, often because they were confined to the home to take care of children. A woman had to leave it to her husband to represent the family at political rallies or meetings. A man's politics were usually his family's politics. Radio brought politics into the home and women into politics.

Radio made it easier for people to react to the qualities and tactics of the politician. Even when a political speaker at a meeting is boring, a member of the audience often feels too self-conscious or too exposed to get up and walk out. Radio gives the listener options: He can listen to the candidates who interest him and avoid those who bore him. In 1924, a writer in *Collier's* magazine remarked that when a radio listener wants to escape political "blah," he simply "raises a languid thumb and forefinger, turns the dial one tenth of an inch, and the blah is gone, but he remembers the blah-er and he will remember him on election day." Likewise, in the 1920s the Milwaukee *Journal* insisted that "whatever makes the candidate speak less and more to the point will improve government."

Radio, and then television, drew our attention away from issues and caused us to focus on the more personal qualities of the candidate, his ability to speak, and his style of presentation. In the 1920s, presidential candidate John W. Davis said that ultimately "a candidate may be chosen for two things: first, that he films well, and second, that he has a good radio voice." Mr.

Davis overstated the case, but he did recognize the intimate nature of the radio medium. His opponent, Calvin Coolidge, was also aware of the personal and emotional aspect of broadcasting, for it was he (despite his reputation as a cold fish) who first put some heart into politics. President Coolidge closed the final radio address of his reelection campaign with the words, "To my father, who is listening in my old home in Vermont, and to my other invisible audience, I say good night."

Too personal? Perhaps. But the New York *Times* remarked that Coolidge's words "counted for merit to an astonishing degree, not with a few, especially women, and a searcher of hearts probably would discover that they won for the President more than a few votes."

Radio also cut out the politician's "silver tongue." The radio audience didn't want oratory, because oratory was uncomfortable in the living room. (FDR sensed that his audience preferred a chat to an oration.) The audience wanted to feel that the speaker was in their parlor, just talking things over.

Before radio, political parties motivated the voter to go out and vote for the ticket. Sometimes a party would use the promise of work or the threat of withholding work. The party machinery was organized to pick up the voters and carry them to the polls via horse and carriage, car, or bus. Before radio, a candidate without a party structure behind him was helpless. But radio could bring the voter out of his house and send him to the polls. The real need of the candidate became not the party structure but the building of another structure that could raise money to buy time on the media. Television added another dimension: the element of visual communication. And so today the major political influences in the country are no longer the Democratic and Republican parties. The major political influences are ABC, CBS, and NBC. They are the organizations that link the voters to politicians and candidates.

Today, in judging candidates, voters do not look for political labels. They look for what they consider to be good character: qualities such as conviction, compassion, steadiness, the willingness to work hard. That is why we have so large a party-crossover vote. This emphasis on people and feeling is the product of an instant-information communication environment.

Today it is far more important for a candidate to use radio and television properly than it is to receive a party's support. We had an example of this in the New Jersey primaries of 1978, when a media campaign helped a political newcomer, former basketball star Bill Bradley, win an easy victory over the party-backed candidate in the race for a senatorial nomination in New Jersey.

In a political campaign today two major questions are

—How do the radio and television stations reach the voting public?

—How do their patterns interface with the election districts?

Politicians often face curious anomalies in dealing with the media. A man running for mayor of Palisades, New Jersey, a small town just across the river from New York City, cannot use television. Since New Jersey has no local television station, New York becomes his "local" station. A New York television station reaches about 15 million people in New York, New Jersey, and Connecticut, but he needs to reach only a few thousand people in one of these states. Furthermore, the rates of the New York stations are the highest in the world.

This lack of co-terminality is an inherent problem in the political use of the electronic media. Election districts are based on a geographic count of population. Media audiences are based on an electronic dispersal system. The two do not, of course, coincide. The average congressional district takes in approximately five hundred thousand people. A television station in New York can reach 12 to 15 million people, or even more. An individual candidate does not even have to reach the five hundred thousand people who constitute his congressional district. He need reach only that proportion of the population eligible to vote, but he is forced to buy more of an audience than he wants.

In rural parts of the country a given station may not even reach all the people in one congressional district, and a candidate who wants the greatest exposure possible will have to buy time on more than one outlet. Yet the cost of air time on stations in such an area is quite small compared to the cost on the media mountain that is New York City. (A radio commercial that may cost four dollars to run once on a small Missouri station could cost two hundred fifty dollars on a New York station.)

Television has made millions feel that they can influence government and public affairs *without participating in politics*. This also means that they believe they can exert influence *without voting*. This belief is not fanciful.

The Watergate hearings were of great importance not only because of the information revealed but also because of the size and response of the television audience. That audience became a political force whose power had nothing to do with the ballot box. Richard Nixon resigned his office, but in a very real sense television and the television audience impeached him before his resignation.

People don't stay home on Election Day merely because they are not good citizens. Many stay at home because they feel that

the ballot box doesn't influence government and public affairs. But that doesn't necessarily cut them off from the political process. Watching and reacting to certain key events on television enables them to have an effect on government. Their reactions are quickly measured by polls, to which politicians pay close attention.

Issues such as wage-price controls, nuclear power, and gas rationing are bigger than most elections—these issues are more important than the specific people who decide them. The public feels this, and that is one of the reasons that only very close elections, or elections involving such highly emotional issues as abortion or gun control, pull out the electorate today.

In spite of this, the media campaign is now the heart and soul of any candidate's run for the roses. This being so, it is inevitable that in the heat of the struggle, candidates misuse the media at times. An election is a competition among men and women who are applying to us, the public, for a job. The candidate running for President or governor or mayor wants us to choose him or her as manager of our "company," "cooperative," or "community." When a candidate is able to convince enough people that he wants what they want, they hire him by electing him to office.

For some mysterious reason, the media and many people share the belief that debate will make the candidates' position on issues clear to us, educate us, equip us to make a rational choice among them. In the world of today's media, the opposite is often true. We can come away from these debates with a feeling for one candidate or another, but that feeling may have nothing to do with the candidate's stand on major issues. It may come from a reaction to the way the candidate presents himself, or from a careless remark he happened to make, or even from the way he looks. Many people believe that if the Nixon-Kennedy debates had been held only on radio, Nixon would have been the winner, but most agreed that Kennedy's physical appearance on television was more engaging than Nixon's. In the Ford-Carter debates, Ford made his careless remark about Poland being a free nation, and that hurt him with the electorate. In the Carter-Reagan debates, Reagan's professional background, not as a politician but as an actor, helped him immeasurably.

Debates claim to give the candidates "thoughtful time" to speak out on the issues, but this turns out to be anywhere from thirty to one hundred twenty seconds to answer such questions as "How will you reorganize the economy?" "What do you think are the most important issues we face? What will you do about them?" "How are you going to deal with crime, education, unemployment?" On a 30- or 60-second radio and television spot, a candidate is given similar time to make a statement on some aspect of the campaign, but hours and hours of thinking can go into the preparation of those 30- and 60-second spots. To prepare them, the candidate does not have to think on his feet, and he has the assistance of political writers, strategists, researchers, and producers.

The net effect of these debates and other conflict-oriented free coverage (news, commentaries, etc.) is to focus on the candidate's problems instead of on the voters' problems and to discourage the turnout of voters on Election Day by turning the election process into a game show whose winners will be announced on election night. This situation impels the candidate to rely on a significant number of paid commercials designed to associate him with the concerns of the voters. The professionals he calls upon to work for him have an impact on his campaign. When David Garth, a prominent political campaign consultant, associated himself with John Anderson's presidential campaign, it increased Anderson's credibility and gave him a better start as a candidate.

During the 1977 New York City mayoralty election, the deficiencies of the debate form on radio and television became so obvious in the primaries that most of the press remarked how alike all the candidates sounded on all important issues. Candidates discussed the budget in terms that few people could understand, and from night to night they began to adopt each other's positions as they gauged public reaction to them. Percy Sutton, one of the major Democratic Party candidates for mayor, told me that "the candidates have seen the need to cater to the editorial writers, the corporate heads, and those who are the opinion molders. . . . You seldom get time enough to come forth with anything of substance."

The media tend to accentuate financial imbalances among the candidates. The wealthy candidate, or the candidate with access to a large pool of support money, has a tremendous advantage, because he can buy more media time and literally make his name a household word. Until recently, corporations and wealthy individuals could wield political power through financial support of a candidate. The new election funding laws have curbed these contributions to a great extent.

With the introduction of the media into politics, a campaign takes on new dimensions and forms, and meets new difficulties. Yet the benefits appear to outweigh the drawbacks: The candidate must speak more directly and cogently or the listener will get bored and turn him off; the candidate has access to all those

who are able to vote, not just his party people; the candidate
can interest young people in the political process even before
they are eligible to vote.

Recently Congress has allowed its sessions to be televised.
Many cable franchises carry the program on a regular basis, and
the results are likely to be startling. We may soon witness the
evolution of a very new type of politician, who will base his career on these changes in the media environment.

The Greeks considered four thousand the ideal number of
people for a participatory democracy. Media coverage of
Congress will raise that number into many millions and bring a
new meaning to our concept of representative government. In
the presence of TV cameras, congressmen may become more
emotional, exhibit more feeling and less detachment. Absen-
teeism, dozing during sessions, and other irresponsible behavior
on the House floor will diminish. Members of Congress will act
more as advocates than as representatives, because we are
watching them.

The work that members of Congress do will become their
campaigns: They will run for reelection from the floor of the
House or the Senate. The speeches they make in their home districts will have to jibe with the speeches they make in Washington. We will be able to measure our representatives against the
best in the country, not just against their opposition at home.

Leaders of a televised Congress will be different from today's
congressional leaders. A representative who has participated in
many house debates seen on TV may not have to campaign as
strenuously as his challenger. Speeches will be shorter if only because viewers can silence a bore by touching an electronic dial.
A representative's competition will come not only from his colleagues but also from other television shows. The House majority leader may be up against "The Guiding Light."

The nature of the television medium that will bring Congress
into our homes is such that it will change what is considered
content. We look to the written word for the communication of
facts and issues, but the television medium is more emotional
and appeals to different interests. This will be disturbing to
many people, but they will be powerless to do anything about it.

As we watch and listen to our representatives, we will learn more about their character than we could by merely reading their words. Bringing Congress into the home will create a new interest in government and inspire more people to seek political careers. Political science may become the hottest course in school.

Televised sessions of Congress will increase public involvement and evoke quicker reactions. Telephone calls to Congress will increase as letters to Congress decrease. The Congressional Record may be available on videotape and computer. Television listings will include the congressional agenda, so that we can tune in to those debates that most interest us. Everyone in the country will be able to know what Congress is doing as it is doing it.

Before long someone will suggest instantaneous polling of the public during House sessions. Viewers will be able to phone two or three separate numbers to indicate their opinion on an issue. A computer will instantly tabulate the votes and display them on the floor of the House. This is now technically feasible.

POLITICAL TV SPOTS SHOULD BE BANNED

This headline appeared over an article in the New York *Times* (Aug. 6, 1978) by David R. Altman, of the Altman-Stoller, Weiss advertising agency.

Headlines very much like that appear regularly in the New York *Times* whenever election season rolls around. Ed Ney, president of Young & Rubicam, has attacked political advertising. So has John O'Toole, president of Foote, Cone, & Belding. The essence of all these attacks is the charge that television advertising trivializes the election process.

But many large agencies oppose political advertising for reasons that have nothing to do with politics, and today few of them represent political clients. Political advertising is like a game. It has winners and losers. It makes news in the community and it generates great emotional involvement. It compresses intense activity into a relatively short span of time, and this disrupts normal advertising schedules. Because political advertising is very absorbing and time-consuming for those members of the agency who work at it, it impedes their work on their product commercials. Political advertising is also highly competitive. Candidates challenge each other's positions. They attack each other and defend themselves. They debate. The advertising community has traditionally shunned this type of fight, and they would not like to see it influence product advertising. In addition, the demands political advertising makes for radio and television air time put it into conflict with commercial advertising. And so it may be that those agencies which oppose political television spots are showing more concern for themselves than for the health of the republic.

But, to return to Mr. Altman's article. In it he wrote, "Television has become the most destructive political force we have ever known." Why? Well, among other reasons, ". . . political ads on TV perform what I consider to be a massive confidence job on the American people." He adds that 30- and 60-second spot announcements should be banned in political campaigns. "There is no way that a candidate can get his ideas across to the television viewers in so short a time."

It is not difficult to argue the opposite point of view: that television has become a constructive political force. Television instantaneously informs the entire country about political developments. More people observe the candidates in commercials than ever before in history.

Mr. Altman would ban the 30- and 60-second spot announcements in favor of longer political statements from candidates. But it took only three or four seconds for candidate Dwight D. Eisenhower to say, "If elected, I will go to Korea"—one of the most effective campaign statements ever made. Polls and the subsequent election testified to the effectiveness of that statement. It told people what they wanted to hear. It gave them promise of a forceful effort to bring a war to a conclusion. It was a total message convincingly spoken by a man who had credibility with the public. In contrast, just recall the boring political speeches you have sat through at town meetings at which politicians took forty minutes to convey nothing.

Suppose we were to substitute 5- or 10-minute time segments for the current 30- and 60-second spots. How many television stations in the country would sell a candidate five or ten minutes of prime time? And how many will sell five or ten minutes of non-prime time? Stations have consistently resisted parting with such time slots, except for presidential candidates.

Mr. Altman further notes that creators of political commercials "use trickery—trick lighting, trick makeup, a full gamut of Hollywood special effects. . . ." Perhaps a few advertising agencies resort to these techniques in political commercials, but the established television producers who specialize in such commercials rarely employ gimmicks. I have used a makeup person only once in the past six years, and that was for candidate Jimmy Carter, who needed a slight touch-up to cover some sunburn peeling. That was an exception to my rule of using no makeup on candidates. I have checked with other producers of political commercials. Like me, they rarely use makeup on their clients.

Although many people think that politicians are sold like soap, I wouldn't even sell soap the way the agencies sell soap. In politics, the better political commercial producers are dealing with communication, not advertising. Here let me examine two political commercials in which I was involved, so that we may see whether it is possible to communicate successfully within the confines of the 30- or 60-second political message.

In the last election, Warren Rudman, a former Republican attorney general in New Hampshire, challenged the incumbent, Democratic Senator John Durkin. After the campaign started, Rudman made an appointment with me to discuss whether I would be interested in doing his commercials. The day before that appointment, Senator John Durkin called me for the same reason. I told the senator that I had an appointment with his opponent, but he said he would like to see me anyway. Since I had made no commitment to Rudman, I met with Durkin that same afternoon.

Although I developed no particular feeling for or against him, I wanted to wait until my meeting with Warren Rudman the next day before deciding which campaign offer to accept. When I met with him he impressed me as a likable man, although I know that first impressions may often be faulty. I asked Rudman what he felt would be the character of his race against Durkin, and he replied that Durkin had already made charges against him that were utterly false. Rudman had asked Durkin to withdraw those charges, but this Durkin declined to do. Rudman asked me to work for him, but I had still not made up my mind.

When John Durkin called me again, I asked whether the charges he had leveled against Rudman were true. Durkin answered by saying that I must know how things are in politics. That answer made up my mind for me, and that very moment I knew that I would accept Warren Rudman's offer. In a campaign, I consider that part of my work is to fight against my candidate's opponent. I don't mind fighting hard, but I never want to fight dirty, because both my reputation and the reputation of my client are on the line.

Following that decision, I was amazed at the number of congressmen, senators, organizations, and officials of one kind or another who called to urge me to work for John Durkin. I can only conclude that Durkin had called on them to put pressure on me not to work for a Republican candidate, but I was comfortable with my decision, even more so when a close friend in Washington, who knows the political ropes very well and who had had experience with both men, agreed with my decision and said, "We need good Republicans here as well as good Democrats."

The campaign proceeded. In the course of working with Warren Rudman I got to like him. On the Wednesday before Election Day, John Durkin, true to form, used the media to air four new commercials, all containing false charges against Rudman. With only five days left, the Durkin camp doubtless figured that we would have no time to answer those commercials with commercials of our own. But, in political campaigns, I have always geared myself and those who work with me to be able to make an almost instantaneous response to any event affecting my candidate. I received copies of the Durkin commercials the same day they were first broadcast. We wrote our answering commercial, a 60-second radio spot, and had it on the air by Thursday morning.

Here is the radio spot:

You've heard the expression "Well, desperate men do desperate things," haven't you? Well, that's the way Senator Durkin seems to be behaving at this point. He sees the election slipping away from him and he feels cornered, so he's making charges against Warren Rudman that are totally false. He charges that Rudman would allow heating-oil prices to go up, when, in fact, Rudman has proposed a freeze on home heating oil. He says Rudman has taken money from oil companies, when in fact he has taken none. But John Durkin has taken two hundred and fifty thousand dollars, that's one quarter of a million dollars, from the special interests. And John Durkin has Exxon's public-relations man doing his fund raising in Washington. We can say only one thing: to the public, "Don't be fooled"; and to Senator Durkin, "Shame on you, John."

At that time I was working with Nurit Karlin, who illustrated this book. She did a drawing for me for our television response to the Durkin commercials, and this commercial was on the air Friday midday, Saturday, Sunday, and Monday, the day before the elections. In the spot, we used Karlin's clever drawing of Pinocchio's head. The nose, of course, grew and grew as the announcer mentioned each of Durkin's misrepresentations. Here are the announcer's words:

Do you remember how Pinocchio's nose would grow whenever he would say something that wasn't true? Well, have you looked at John Durkin lately? Twice John Durkin said that Warren Rudman took money from big oil company executives. Both times that wasn't true and he knew it. And now, when Warren Rudman wants to freeze heating-oil prices so we won't freeze this winter, John Durkin says that Rudman wants to deregulate those prices. And that isn't true. . . . Shame on you, John.

Here is what Rudman himself had to say about the Pinocchio commercial after it had run for only two days:

We've been using television, of course, for the primary, and we used it for a number of weeks in the general. Now we get into these last few days and out comes this Pinocchio spot, which had to be produced on four or five hours' notice and flown up and put on stations. It played Friday night, it played some on Saturday, and a fair amount on Saturday night. I walk into factories on Monday morning and I realize something very strange was happening. From time to time people would tell me that our commercials are good. Now all of a sudden people are starting to say, "Hey, I saw that Pinocchio cartoon. That's a marvelous political commercial.

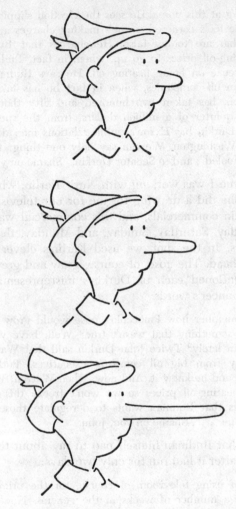

My wife and I chuckled. What a terrific way to call a guy a liar!"
. . . Every third or fourth person I'd shake hands with in these factories would talk about Pinocchio. When any television commercial
has that kind of impact, after being lightly exposed for only forty-
eight hours, all I got to tell you is that we sure did something right.

Warren Rudman defeated incumbent Senator John Durkin
handily.

The New
Grammar

We are all used to hearing the plaintive cry "Johnny can't read! Johnny can't write!" This distresses Johnny's elders, who grew up believing that literacy is the basic attribute, the *sine qua non*, for anyone with even a pretense to culture. Well, it's true that many schoolchildren have severe reading and writing problems. Those who attempt to analyze these difficulties point a finger gleefully at television and brand it as the culprit: "Johnny and Jane are spending all their leisure time mesmerized by the idiot tube. They're becoming television zombies."

Here we come across a curious contradiction. It seems safe to assume that because television has reduced our dependence on reading, many children today have been slower to develop reading and writing skills. At the same time, television is probably one of the best reading-readiness tools ever devised. An illiterate child can learn from television many things that a literate adult can learn from reading, and most reading theoreticians agree that children find it easier to learn to read if they are familiar with the subject they are reading about.

In years past, the duty of a child, to know and grow, was in reality the province only of the children of the nobility, and later of the upper class. Today electronic media have taken a giant step in the democratization of the process of knowing and growing. They have broken through the print barrier. Radio and television have made the process available to virtually all the children in this country, rich and poor alike.

In classes on anthropological and sociological documentation where I've used tape recorders and cameras, I've found that the age of a student has little relation to his ability to learn. Once a child has reached the age of eight or nine, I have no difficulty incorporating him into a class of adults. Conversely, I find no difficulty in incorporating adults into a class of children.

In the late 1960s, Donald Barr, then the director of the Dalton School, established a class for school pupils who were considered poor readers and poor listeners. I led the class. The pupils ranged in age from nine to fourteen. Then a number of adults asked to participate in the class. They included nursery-school teachers in their mid-twenties, a man from the Poughkeepsie school system in his mid-forties, and Dr. Marshall McLuhan, who was then in his late fifties. We taught things the students were interested in: current events, the art and science of sound, the relation of hearing to reading and writing, tape editing, and even philosophy. We were all both teachers and learners. The most important achievement of the class was to make clear the relationship of listening to reading and writing. One device that accomplished this quite directly was a project that required each student to prepare a biography in sound. In doing this project, the recording of interviews and the editing of tapes demanded thinking, structuring, and listening.

Though not in a conscious manner, Johnny and Jane are today learning a new and very sophisticated grammar, the grammar of film and television. For instance, let us imagine that Johnny and Jane are watching an old movie, perhaps a Charlie Chan picture in which Charlie travels from Hong Kong to New York. The old film shows Charlie and his Number One Son boarding a ship in Hong Kong. Next follow a series of shots of the ship's silhouette on the ocean and perhaps a view aboard the ship. Finally, the ship steams past the Statue of Liberty, pulls into New York Harbor, and docks at a West Side midtown pier. Charlie comes on deck and walks down the gangplank, followed by his son. Any child of seven or eight who watches this sequence of suggestive images knows that the Chans have reached New York.

The grammar of modern films and television is more sophisticated and elliptical. People in film and television now travel by swish pan or by a simple device such as a doorknob. A hero will be in a room in Paris. He has to go to New York. The camera may pull in to the doorknob on the door of his Paris hotel, and then pull back from a doorknob in New York, and the hero has traveled! Everybody in our society understands this. We no longer have to show various stages of the entire trip. Yet people in parts of the world that television and film have not yet reached would never conclude from those doorknob shots that Charlie and his son had traveled. There are still people in isolated areas of the globe who do not understand that a photograph of a person is a representation of that person.

Today we can tune in a popular sports program on television and see a mile race in California, cut to a weight-lifting contest in Moscow, cut to a soccer match in Brazil, then to a gymnastic tournament in China. All of the events come to us "live" and now. What's more, Johnny and Jane understand this quite readily.

We are familiar with scenes on television and in the movies wherein we hear dialogue without seeing the people. The camera gives us a long shot of a car driving along a highway. Though we cannot see them, we know that two people are inside, and we hear their dialogue and readily accept the scene as realistic. Years ago such a technique would have seemed bizarre or even ridiculous, but to Johnny and Jane it seems perfectly normal.

All the media have a cross-influencing effect, and the new grammar of film and television has entered the style of many writers. (If you compare a number of novels written over the past fifty years, you will find on the average far more dialogue and paragraphing in the more recent books.) Pauline Kael, reviewing the motion-picture version of the novel *Bloodbrothers*, made this comment:

> Many novelists have been influenced by the movies, but probably no "serious" novelist has absorbed into his writing what movie audiences want the way that Richard Price, the young author of *Bloodbrothers*, has. (He was twenty-five when he wrote the book.) He describes the action—bam-pow—and tells the story through dialog; the effect is like that of a classic novel speeded up. It's a childish approach to the novel, but that of a TV-age child aware that he's competing with movies and TV for your attention and determined not to lose you for an instant. (*The New Yorker*, Oct. 2, 1978)

Before we accept the accusation that television has made Johnny and Jane slow learners, we must first consider how television has changed the relationship of reading to our lives. For most of us, learning to read was the first step toward learning to learn. Without the ability to read, one couldn't know about the world beyond the hill or the thinking that went on beyond that hill. Today everything beyond the hill and behind the moon comes into our homes and minds, bypassing the school and library. We are living in a world in which the dominant form of communication is acoustical and visual in nature, and yet we castigate our youngsters because, unlike their parents, they didn't grow up in a print-dominated world.

We must accept the fact that television has changed the context of reading in our lives today. The first years of a child's education were once devoted to providing that child with the ability to read. The child needed to read in order to be able to learn. Today, without knowing how to read, a child can still learn from radio, television, telephone, tape, and film. Although some may feel that certain media are superior to others, an individual can often have the choice of reading a story, hearing a story read, or seeing a film or television production of that story. A child can now learn to read closer to the time when he needs to read, that is, when he is old enough to enter many areas of knowledge that are specialized and not carried as common, everyday experience on electronic media.

We who were raised to appreciate books find it difficult, even repellant, to accept the fact that *the need to read and write is not as urgent as it was before the electronic media.* Even before radio and television, the telephone reduced the need to read and write. The art of letter writing, once highly developed by many cultivated people, has atrophied almost to the point of extinction, largely because of the telephone.

This is not a defense of illiteracy or a claim that the ability to read and write brings with it no advantage. What I am suggesting is that since we have so many other ways of learning today, we must reexamine all our pedagogical theories about how and when to teach reading and writing.

Reading primers for children often contain simple pictures to go along with the words. Beneath a full-page drawing of a chair will be the word "chair" in both upper- and lower-case letters. The illustration helps connect the child's experience to the printed word. Why, then, do we make so little use of television as a reading-readiness tool? Why do educators persist in damning television as the enemy of reading, rather than using it as a learning device? Probably because teachers, biased by the attempt to link television with illiteracy, do not consider it a valid part of a child's experience. They put reading and writing in one compartment, and television in another, and treat them as mutually incompatible. But there is nothing inherently incompatible about them.

A teacher will ask a child to write about his summer vacation, a game he played, or about some little artifact he displayed during a show-and-tell session, assuming that all these are part of a child's experience. But television is at least as much a part of a child's experience as any of these things. How often are children asked to watch a specific program and then write about it? Why do teachers seldom encourage the discussion of a television series unless it comes with that dreadful epithet "educational," or assign pupils to review a television program? News, current-events shows, and political campaigns all relate to social studies. Television coverage of the Mount St. Helens eruption made a splendid adjunct to geological studies. In the past few years, young people have been able to learn about the treasures of King Tutankhamen, Colombian art, and the paintings of Picasso because of television coverage of these art works as they appeared in exhibitions all over the country. How many teachers discuss with their pupils television shows or specials? Do they ever abstract for the purpose of learning or memorizing some twenty words that identify articles seen on a particular television show, articles on such as an oil rig, a suction pump, a cable car, a jet engine, an unfamiliar animal?

In publications such as *TV Guide*, teachers can find listings of future television shows together with brief descriptions of their content, determine which of these might deal with matters that interest the students, and work out studies relating to these shows. Teachers can utilize television shows as a source of experience common to all their pupils.

It can even be argued that television encourages reading.

One example out of thousands: After WABC-TV ran its television motion picture series *Rich Man, Poor Man,* based on an Irwin Shaw novel, publishers reissued the novel in paperback. The television show had created a new reading audience. The sales of Shakespeare plays increase after any Public Television Shakespeare performance. The televised version of Alex Haley's *Roots* boosted the sales of the book. Every television adaptation of a literary work, no matter what its quality, encourages reading simply by publicizing the book.

There are, of course, areas of learning that television cannot provide. Advanced students who want to become specialists in ancient Greek history or the religion of Islam would most certainly have to learn about these things from books and possibly from the direct use of other media such as film and tape recordings in the classroom. But when we are dealing with small children in the early stages of learning we are talking of the study of material now common to all. We are talking about the general areas of life around us and what is happening in the world. This is information that the electronic media are conveying to all children today. This information tells them about who is running for President, what the weather will be, why the family is curtailing automobile travel because of the high price of gas, the energy shortage, a flu epidemic, sports results, the number of unemployed, the rate of inflation.

The role of the teacher will be more attuned to reality when the teacher understands how and why the media have made the mastery of reading and writing less urgent to the child. The role of the school is no longer to organize the distribution of information but to teach students how to handle the information that is now common to all—in a word, to teach students to think and to utilize television, radio, reading, writing, any and all forms of communication, as tools in that process. Because we have an overload of information, the school's function is to help students sift through and make use of that flood of information that might otherwise overwhelm them. The role of the teacher should include teaching children how to structure and place in perspective information they already possess and are constantly absorbing. Very few teachers take this approach, and children have paid the price for their failure to do so by becoming uninterested in "school" learning.

Robert Frost said that "education is hanging around until you've caught on." Buckminster Fuller once wrote, "Human beings have developed words so that we can communicate our experience: that's what education is." He went on to say that in the modern world each successive child is being born in the presence of more reliable information. Fuller was not worried about whether children get that information through reading, looking at cartoons, or sitting in front of a television set. Said Fuller, "The kids are going to latch on to whatever it may be," and, "The fact is that latching on to TV is really a most wonderful thing. An apparent problem is that we're using it as a means to make money—to sell toothpaste, and so on. The kids, however, aren't really so much interested in that information, but just in the way the thing is working. They love the technique; they're studying the technique all the time. They take in the use of language much more than they do the message."

As Frost might have put it, the real question is "How do we hang around other people's thinking?" The medium we hang around in is not important.

Teachers are, in a sense, "paid media." We purchase their time to structure the unpaid media. In my political advertising I have always used paid media to structure the unpaid media, news programs and the like, which broadcast all sorts of information. The paid media enable me to put that information in what I consider its proper context in terms of the candidate for whom I am working. Similarly, when a teacher is dealing with large areas of common knowledge and information, his role is to put things in their proper context.

Fundamentally, the relationship between reading and television is no more antagonistic than the relationship between the horse and the automobile. The horse and the automobile are not angry at each other. It's the equestrians who get angry at the automobile, and the print-oriented teachers who get angry at television, when in fact peaceful coexistence is possible.

The Electronic Classroom

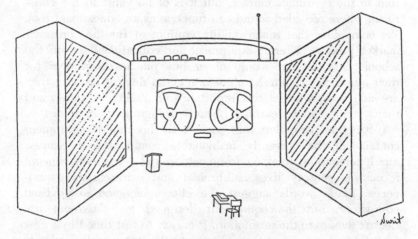

We generally assume that vision dominates the senses, yet this dominance is by no means innate. It is the result of five hundred years of the visual domination in communication that began with Gutenberg. For five hundred years, all communication other than conversation or speeches took the form of the written or printed word. Not surprisingly, our educational system has inherited a bias in favor of anything related to the printed visual, and a reluctance to fully employ auditory technology in the classroom. In recent years, many educational institutions have put money into audiovisual documentation but pinched the pennies when it came to audio documentation. For years, Professor Alan Nevins, of Columbia University, directed an oral-history project. He recorded hundreds of people prominent in politics, literature, music, science, and other fields. Associates transcribed these recordings and then destroyed them. They were using these valuable recordings as nothing more than a dictation service. Many years later, the pressure exerted by people like Dr. Victor Witten, a collector of auditory documentation, finally persuaded Professor Nevins to preserve his sound recordings.

Almost without exception, the entire educational field has tended to equate sound with the cassette and its small speaker. Drugstores offer sight-and-sound toys and devices for children for less than thirty-five dollars. Perhaps this kind of junk can be sold in the consumer market, but it is of no value in the classroom, where recorded sound can function as an educational tool. Yet companies that make quality equipment for the consumer market produce inferior equipment for educational use in the schools. Schools that would never buy plastic saxophones for their music classes purchase cut-rate audio devices because they are simply unaware of the importance of quality in sound, and they are not open to learning, because of ingrained prejudices.

Instruction pamphlets that come with this shoddy equipment contain all the currently fashionable communication words: aural perception, total environment, spatial reasoning, concept formation, sensory lives, subliminal and extrasensory experiences. These words suggest the effects of good audiovisual equipment, but the equipment designed for classroom use doesn't live up to the promotion. It is easy to test this. Buy a few high-fidelity and some stereo demonstration tapes and records of sound effects. Play one of the records on a child's forty-nine dollar phonograph with its one- to three-watt amplifier, which gives it the same quality as the equipment made for the schools. You will have difficulty identifying the orchestral instruments and really experiencing the emotionality of the music. Now play the same record on a quality high-fidelity system. The contrast is astounding.

Now take the stereo demonstration tape, cut out the words identifying the sound effects, and splice these sounds on a reel of tape with short sections of leader tape between them. Rerecord these sounds on a battery-operated recorder costing under sixty dollars. Play the new tape for some friends and ask them to identify the sound. Next, thread the original tape on a quality tape deck and play it through a high-fidelity sound system. When you play the rerecorded tape on a cheap, portable unit, six or seven people out of ten may not be able to identify the sound, but when you play the original tape on good equipment, only one or two people in ten will fail to identify a particular sound.

I tried this experiment with fifty students. The words they used to describe the inferior sound were "fuzzy," "not clear," "confused," "distant," "thin," "weak," "remote." In describing the high-quality sound, they used phrases such as "It's the real thing," "I'm more involved in it," "I know what it is," "I can feel it," "I'm there with it." There is a close relationship between the quality of sound and our emotional reaction to it.

When educators supply the classroom with those crude 1- to 3-watt amplifiers, in contrast to the 20- to 200-watt systems many of the children have at home, it is no wonder that the kids aren't attentive. There is an even greater contrast between the low-power equipment and the 50- to 100-watt guitar amplifiers that increasing numbers of teenagers own. The inferior audio equipment in the schools muddles rather than develops perception. Although some may blame this situation on a lack of finances, schools don't buy junk when they really value a piece of equipment.

Put the sound of a running horse on a small cassette recorder, and whoever listens to it will be hard put to recognize what he is hearing. Play the hum of a mosquito and the sound of a propeller plane at the same volume on this small cassette and you cannot tell one from the other. Since the student cannot readily identify sounds on this inferior equipment, the teacher or narrator on the recording falls back on words and tells the student what he is going to hear. The sound that most students are exposed to is primarily *narrated* sound. It is sound effects, not the effect of sound.

Where we would expect to find the most imaginative use of the new tape technology, we find the most stodgy and dated approach. Schools use tape and cassette programs that are not creatively constructed originals but merely copies of other environments. Tapes and cassettes are misused as containers for older media: print and lectures. These programs make little use of the temporal and spatial potential of tape.

Educators have not yet realized that they can edit tape to mold actual recordings of political, social, and scientific events into important historical units that reveal patterns of change and effects. Perhaps it is because the recording and editing of audio and videotape are not yet part of a teacher's training. Most publishers use tapes as a means of presenting a fully packaged class, rather than providing shorter tapes that can evoke response and inspire discussion. Educators err when they use tapes almost exclusively as a finished package for passive listening.

The average cassette used in the classroom takes up the same amount of time as the scheduled class itself. But what is the point of using a new medium to perform the function of an old one? The real value of the new media in the schools is to bring to the student *material that cannot be seen or heard in any other way*.

How much more valuable would be a cassette of any length that offers material or evidence that evokes discussion, rather than ends it. Consider the field of family relations. A cassette can offer students a lecture on the subject, a résumé of some of the problems every family encounters, a comparison of the nuclear versus the extended family. A lecture or a pamphlet can do the same. But what can the cassette offer that is unique? It can offer a recording of an honest-to-God family fight, so that everyone in the class can hear and discuss the evidence of real life.

I am familiar with a tape produced by a manufacturer of medical supplies. On it a manic-depressive speaks for about a minute. Then a doctor introduces himself and gives a talk on manic depression and the palliative effects of some drugs on persons so afflicted. The only unique thing that the cassette could offer, the only thing that could not be heard in any other way, was the voice of the manic-depressive, who, had she talked for the entire length of the tape, might have made the audience aware of the special qualities and mode of communication associated with this ailment. That would have provided listeners with a learning experience that only a tape or a face-to-face encounter could offer.

I once produced a tape through a rather unfortunate set of

circumstances: I received a long-distance call from a friend. The moment he started to speak, I could tell he was suicidal, and indeed he told me he was about to throw himself out of the nineteenth-floor hotel room he was occupying. Luckily I was with another friend. I told this friend to call the police in the town where my caller was staying and direct them to his hotel. Then I gave myself the task of keeping my caller on the phone until the police arrived. My phone can be hooked up to a recorder which I turn on when I want to record information instead of taking notes. I recorded my conversation with him.

I was able to keep him talking until the police arrived. When I hung up, I had a tape of special value and quality. That tape was subsequently played to the psychiatrist who treated my severely depressed friend. Tapes like this one can also be of use to medical and psychiatric students. The tape was not a description of symptoms, it was an *exhibition* of symptoms. It was, as they say, the "real thing." Cassettes can bring the "real thing" into the classroom.

A revolution is soon to come in the field of education: the revolution in the library. This revolution is not yet here, but it is very close at hand. The library is, of course, the place where we keep books. But, with the rapid development of computerized print transmission, we may soon have no need for the library as it is now constructed. The library of the future will be an electronic center containing tapes or magnetic disks with lines connected to video outputs. It won't be necessary to physically remove a cassette for home use, since the "borrower" will be electronically connected to this library, and a playing device there will feed the sound of that cassette into the home, the office, or the school. For example, you may want to request a certain speech of Franklin D. Roosevelt's. To do this, you'll need only to dial a code number on a push-button phone, and FDR's voice will come out of your hi-fi speaker. You can play all of the cassette or any section of it. You can replay certain passages as often as you please just by touching your Touch-Tone telephone.

For purposes of study, research, and simple enjoyment, many people will still want to read rather than listen to some material. Again the new library will oblige. We are now witnessing an explosion in the electronic transmission of the printed word. You can now buy a device that you can attach to your phone. Using this device, you can receive material from any information bank in the world, and it will be printed on a screen in your own home. Soon we will be able to receive in printed form on our television tube any published material: newspaper, newsletter, book, catalog. The new library will be able to "type" this printed material into your television set and provide you, in visual form, with the reading matter of your choice. Your picture tube and your stereo speakers will be your home library. You will no longer go to the library to take something out. The library and its information will come to you.

This new electronic capability suggests that, in many situations, education will soon become part of the work process. You will be able to learn at the moment the need for learning arises. When the need to know exists, education is simpler, more involving, and more lasting. My wife recently plugged in an electric vaporizer to relieve the symptoms of a head cold. The water did not flow into the vaporizer properly and she asked me to fix it. I sat down in front of it, stared at it, cursed it a little, and tried to figure out the mechanical principles on which it was constructed. However, I was not able to discover what was impeding the flow of water. Then my wife located an instruction sheet that came with the machine when we bought it. By studying the sheet, I soon learned that a cap that fitted on the end of a shaft was missing. I fished around in the bottom of the receptacle, found the cap, fitted it on the shaft, and the machine functioned properly. I was getting my education in a situation in which I needed to know. Had I studied that instruction sheet a year ago, when we bought the machine, I would never have been able to absorb the information as effectively as I did when I had an immediate use for it.

This is the kind of instruction that could be fed over a line from a technical library that supplies information for the repair of electronic instruments. Dial-access to knowledge is not a fanciful dream but part of the future. It will become a major process in job training, and it will vastly increase the amount of on-the-job education.

The library, like the school, will one day cease to be a place in which the students spend long periods of time. It will become a studio or transmission center that transmits intensified knowledge much as a magnifying glass gathers and concentrates the heat of the sun. As yet, we cannot know the exact effect of the new technology on the physical, organizational, and time structures of educational establishments, nor can we predict what will be the effects of the new technologies on work patterns and environments. We can only say that they will bring about vast changes as modern education slowly, and somewhat reluctantly, enters the electronic age.

The Incredible
Expanding
Telephone

The telephone is a magical instrument of electronic communication. It has changed the social life of every American community. The communication we receive from our television sets and our home radios is one-way: from the broadcaster to the listener. Telephonic communication allows the sender and the receiver to exchange roles at will.

The traditional use of the telephone is to hold conversations with those who are beyond the range of our unaided voice. In addition, the telephone offers a variety of services, some humorous, some trivial, some useful. We can dial a prayer, a joke, a children's story, weather and sports reports, movie and museum schedules. Tape and computers feed this information into the phone. But we also have people manning telephones for important emergency services: poison centers, suicide hot lines, drug and alcohol guidance, and the like. In Vienna, whose former mayor Köchel once catalogued all the works of Mozart, you can dial a number and receive the musical note A so that you can tune your instrument.

The telephone and the radio have changed the character of the social protection that municipalities can offer their citizens. If you call the police in an emergency, they will relay your call by radio to a police car cruising in your vicinity. The telephone and the radio have also made possible the instant transmission of information about fire and medical emergencies.

Mount Sinai Hospital in New York City has set up a telephone lecture library. Any individual can call in and listen to a prerecorded talk on any one of dozens of medical problems.

The telephone helps us deal with our emotions quickly and directly. If, for instance, I feel that some company in Akron, Ohio, has done me a serious disservice, I don't have to put my feelings down in a letter and then wait for an answer while my anger mounts or fades. I can pick up the phone, express myself, get instant business and emotional satisfaction, and quickly regain my mental equilibrium.

The telephone is replacing older means of providing services. Over the past few years, we have suffered from a steady deterioration of our mail service. Fifty years ago the public would not have tolerated such deterioration, but we accept it today with a minimum of grumbling, because of the telephone. We know that as a last resort the telephone can probably get us any information we really need. We can even transmit printed material by phone. A secretary can type a letter on a computer or typewriter and have it "zapped" by phone in seconds to a compatible computer or typewriter anywhere in the world. In the Qwip system, typewritten letters or pictures are attached to a rotating cylinder, electronically scanned on the transmission end, carried over telephone lines, and reproduced on a rotating cylinder at the receiving end. It now takes the Qwip machine a few minutes to scan a page, but the system is being rapidly improved.

The 800-number system, which allows customers to make a toll-free call from anywhere in the country, has become an important commercial service. A woman reads an advertisement for a dress that she can order by calling a toll-free 800 number. Someone at the 800 service number takes her call. When she tells him the dress she wants to order, a computer feeds the information to a cathode ray tube (CRT). The face of the CRT tells the 800 employee what questions to ask: what size? what color? He punches the answers into the computer, then takes the woman's credit-card number. The computer verifies in seconds the credit status of that card number, then provides an order in printout form containing the name and address of the buyer, her credit-card status, and the size and color of the dress. The 800 service delivers the printout to the supplier by the next morning, and the store can immediately ship or mail the dress to the buyer. An individual or company can also use the 800 number to make toll-free calls simply by paying a flat fee for the service.

More recently, the phone company has developed a 900 number, which allows people anywhere in the country to "vote" on questions. A computer keeps a tally of how many people call various prearranged phone numbers to express support for a particular candidate or a stand on a social issue. ABC used the 900 number after the Carter-Reagan debate, and over one million people called in to "vote" for their choice. The results indicated a strong trend toward Reagan—a trend which none of the major pollsters had yet picked up.

The telephone contributes immeasurably to my own work. Today I record many commercials by phone. Regular clients in cities around the country call me in New York to discuss radio commercials that are needed for a given week, or, if they have prepared a rough draft of a commercial, they use the telephone to transmit that draft by Qwip machine. I receive the rough draft in printed form from the Qwip machine attached to my own phone. I go over the draft, making what changes I think are necessary, and my secretary types it up. Then I use my phone to send the copy by Qwip machine to an announcer in California, who records for me.

It takes about five minutes to receive the copy information or suggested copy from the client, fifteen to twenty minutes to correct it and have it typed, and four to six minutes to send it by Qwip machine to California.

In California the announcer receives the script and he is ready to record it on his tape machine. I then telephone him. He and I use speaker phones. I stay on the line while he is recording. Because I can hear him at work, I am able to direct him as he records and ask for changes or different readings. When we are both satisfied with the finished tape, he calls an air-express service. This service picks up the tape at his house, takes it to the Los Angeles airport, and puts it on a plane to New York. The New York office of the air-express service picks up the tape when the plane lands and delivers it to my office.

In other words, I can get a draft of a commercial at four in the afternoon, record it in California, and receive it in recorded form on my desk by eight o'clock the next morning.

You may wonder why I don't speed up the process still further by having my California announcer record the commercial by telephone while I tape it here in my New York office. That is possible technically but not financially. It would require a full-frequency telephone line such as FM stations use to transmit music. Such a full-frequency line, unlike the ordinary telephone line, can transmit the full frequency range of the human voice. However, the installation and balancing of such a special line in the home or office is a very expensive proposition.

I lecture all over the world without leaving my office. I do this by using the portable conference telephone. To receive me, those organizing the lecture must rent this equipment at their end. A portable conference phone, available from any local

phone company, is about the size of a portable typewriter, but it can amplify the telephone call over a built-in speaker system with enough power to reach fifty to seventy-five people in a room. Larger systems are available for larger audiences. I have lectured for groups in Australia, Japan, France, Canada, and other countries and in at least fifteen cities in the United States by telephone. I have addressed students in four or five colleges at once. Another teleconference connected me simultaneously to advertising managers in England, Germany, Holland, Argentina, France, Brazil, Pakistan, Austria, and several other countries. These telelectures allow me to speak and present auditory material, listen to and answer questions, and conduct a two-way dis-

cussion with my audience. I can cue in whatever visual material
I want to display. I forward films or videotapes to wherever I
want to lecture. Using the Touch-Tones on my telephone, I can
start or stop these films or tapes whenever I wish. My telephone
equips me to deliver auditory and visual presentations anywhere
in the world at relatively low cost. Whoever uses such devices is
billed at the regular rate for an ordinary long-distance telephone
call, plus the rental for the conference amplifier. That rental can
be as low as fourteen dollars a month.

Instead of our having to ship our bodies to distant parts, the
telephone allows us to attend conferences and speak or listen
without leaving our rooms. Curiously, the disembodied telephone voice often attracts more attention than the voices of
those who attend in the flesh. I have a friend who went to a conference on advertising in London. I spoke to that conference by
phone, and when my friend returned from London he com-
plained that people paid more attention to my telephone voice
than to his live voice. It's like the old story of the passerby who
comments to a new mother, "My, what a beautiful baby you
have!" to which the mother replies, "Yes, but you should see her
pictures."

My telephone voice attracts the attention it does, not necessarily because my contributions to a conference are superior to
anyone else's. I am a magical spirit who appears out of nowhere.
People have asked me why I do not supply a photograph, some
indication of a body to which an audience can attach my voice.
But I do not believe that is necessary. In some mysterious way,
the telephone involves people very deeply and the photograph is
superfluous. I want people to "see what I mean," not to see me.

The telephone is growing, albeit slowly, as a tool in education.
The Educational Telephone Network, at the University of Wisconsin Extension, uses the phone conference system to link more
than two hundred locations throughout the state. Over thirty
thousand Wisconsin students attend telephone-based courses.

Why haven't educators made much more use of the telephone? Is it because they have not yet devised a way to keep
teachers from making personal calls? Or is that too frivolous a
thought? Consider, for instance, the area of vocational guidance.
Vocational-guidance teachers often invite a guest to talk to stu-

dents about a particular trade or profession. How simple it would be, how efficient, how effective, how time-saving in terms of travel, to supply such classes with telephone hookups and let the students chat with people prominent in various vocations. It is a simple and convenient way to bring specialists into the classroom.

I am writing this the night before I am scheduled to speak on "Politics in Communication" over the national PBS network. The broadcast will originate in Boston. I will talk from New York. My words will reach people in thirty-eight states, all of whom can call in with questions on an 800-number line. I will be transmitting my voice and material instantaneously to an area covering approximately three quarters of this country.

The telephone has become indispensable in market and political research. One company, Richard Dresner Associates, which I mentioned earlier, conducts polls for product manufacturers, newspapers, television stations, and others. These polls are taken in every one of the fifty states. An individual poll covering thousands of people can be completed in two or three days, and no poll taker leaves the Dresner New York offices.

Every day, we see new developments in the field of telephone equipment: answering machines, automatic dialing, speaker phones, feed-out machines to supply callers with recorded information. Private phone companies are now designing sophisticated systems tailored to the specific requirements of offices. These will lead to important changes in life styles and work styles.

The beeper is a small device that I carry with me at all times, attached to my belt or tucked away in my pocket. If an important call comes into my office when I am out, my secretary calls a special number. A radio signal that activates my beeper is then transmitted. If I am driving, I stop my car at the nearest phone booth, call my office, and have myself connected to the caller. Once when I phoned my secretary after I heard my beeper, I learned that she was keeping a call from California on hold. I have a device that can link or "bridge" two telephone lines, and so I was connected from the phone booth on the roadway to the caller in California, all in a matter of minutes. This beeper operates within a radius of ninety-five miles of my office, but companies are now developing beepers that will activate transmitters anywhere in the mainland United States. The cost of this service runs from seven dollars a month if you own the beeper, to twenty-two dollars a month if you rent it.

Another socially important telephone-based service is banking by phone. You can, for instance, pay your bills by phone. You call your bank number and then use the Touch-Tone numbers on your phone to punch in information about the amount of money involved, the number of your account, the date, and other essential information. Instead of transferring paper money from bank to bank, we are now able to make these transfers electrically. This service, along with credit cards, has eliminated the need for paper money, except for a bit of pocket money to purchase a newspaper or a package of cigarettes. Indeed, millions of Americans spend most of their paychecks without exchanging any paper money.

A study has shown that today most face-to-face communication in large offices takes place only when people are less than eighty feet from each other. When the distance is greater, people in offices tend to use the telephone. I had a friend, an advertising agency comptroller, who conducted a simple experiment to determine how much he really needed to go to his office to work. For one week he had all correspondence slipped under his door and spoke to people inside and outside the office by phone. In that entire week he had occasion to open his office door in connection with work only three times! He could have stayed home and done 99 percent of his work on the phone.

The telephone has changed the location of many companies. Years ago, all companies wanted their plants and offices to be in one location to facilitate communication and the collection and dispersal of information. (When we call for telephone or airline information, we are often connected to cities other than the one we are in.) Today the main office of many companies is "main" only because the top executives use it. Companies have decentralized and dispersed their real estate holdings and plant structures, because the telephone makes it possible for these scattered units to function more efficiently than they did when they occupied one location. Companies now determine manufacturing sites by such factors as the availability of raw materials, labor, access to transportation, and the political and social climate. Ampex manufactures parts of the new Ampex recorders in Japan, while the electrical components are built in Mexico. The combination of air travel, electronic imagery, and the ability to communicate instantly assures the company that all its parts will mesh and all its measurements and tolerances will be compatible with each other despite the dispersal of the plant facilities.

In previous eras, executives, most of whose activity involves communication, had to travel to work. Although executives still go to their offices, they could just as well stay home and "communicate to work." I remember receiving a call from a man in San Francisco who wanted to come East for a conference with me. I suggested that aside from being expensive the trip would serve no purpose. We were on the phone. Why didn't we hold our conference then and there? Talking to San Francisco by phone costs a lot less than a round-trip plane ticket, a hotel room, a few restaurant meals, and two days out of the office.

Any new development has its negative aspects. During a severe blizzard in New York City a friend of mine from out of town wanted to take his son to the Museum of Natural History's Laserium for the light show. Because of weather conditions, I was not sure that the Laserium would be open and I offered to check by phone. I looked up the number and called, expecting a quick answer to the simple question "Is the Laserium show on tonight?"

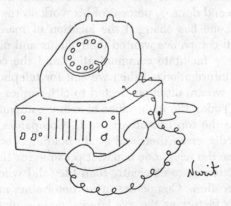

Nurit

No human being answered my call. Instead I heard a tape recording that regaled me with details of a Laser-rock exhibit that promised a dramatically different combination of light show and rock-and-roll music. The nonhuman recording was a radio show in miniature, with sound effects, background music, and a hucksterish voice hawking the glories of the Laserium. Then I learned that if I wanted ticket information I must call 977-9020. For group discounts I was to call 566-0440. And for information about combination tickets I was to call 872-1389. Then the taped voice crooned into my ear, à la Mae West, "Hope to see you here real soon."

This phone call took two minutes and twenty-eight seconds, but it did not answer my question "Is the Laserium show on tonight?" And so I called one of the recommended numbers. No one answered. I dialed again. Another tape responded. The man who spoke on that tape told me that I could get information about the Laserium by calling 724-8700 (the number I originally called); I could learn about astronomical events by calling 873-0404, while a call to 873-5714 would give me details of school shows. And if I was still hungry for further information I could get it by calling 873-1389. It took the tape two minutes and forty-three seconds to read me a description of a sky show and the week's schedule, but my question "Is the Laserium show on tonight?" was still unanswered.

Well, I'm no quitter, so I dialed another recommended number. This time a woman answered (on tape, of course). In two minutes and forty seconds this tape gave me museum information, warned me against taking box lunches with me, told me what school kids should do about reservations, and listed all the metropolitan subway and bus routes to the museum. Then I was told to call 873-1300 for additional information; 873-7320 for reservations; 873-8828 for information about Planetarium shows; and 724-3413 for information about the Laserium.

I am a good citizen and I do as I am told, and so I dialed 724-3413 for Laserium information. An operator answered to ask me what number I wanted. Before I could delight in communicating with a real human being, she pressed a button that connected me with a tape recording that said, "The number you have reached, 723-3413, has been changed. The new number is 724-8700. Please make a note of this." This took one minute and thirty-five seconds. Imagine what it does to phone bills when one tape is used to correct the misinformation on another tape! And what was the corrected number? It was the very first number I called at the beginning of this saga!

I still refused to give up. I went through my list of numbers and chose one I had not yet tried. A miracle occurred. A man answered, a real, live, flesh-and-blood man, and the following conversation took place:

Man

Hello.

Me

Hello. Is the Laserium show on tonight?

Man

Yes, it's on tonight.

Me

Thank you.

End of conversation. Total time elapsed: six seconds. Thanks to the wonders of computer and tape technology, I spent a total of nine minutes and twenty-six seconds (at a cost of $1.20) and got no answer whatsoever to my question "Is the Laserium show on tonight?" During that nine minutes plus of unwanted sound one man shouted at me as though I were across the room, rather than on the phone. I had to listen to people reading scripts or playing roles in mini radio dramas. In nine minutes and twenty-six seconds I could not get a six-second answer.

Properly structured telephone interaction with computers, banks of prerecorded tapes, and other new technologies has the potential of providing many valuable services. But poor design can result in a telephonic disaster.

Communication in
the Year 2000

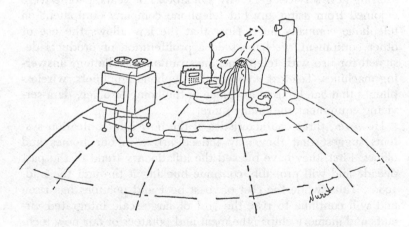

During these last two decades of the century, a broad range of communication technologies will develop and change how many of us work, learn, and use leisure time. We will send and receive electronic mail, talk back to our television sets and be heard by our program host, and participate in electronic business meetings with colleagues who are scattered around the globe. The technological means are not science-fiction dreams; each exists today. However, it will take a number of years for them to be implemented on a large scale.

The new communication systems are fascinating hybrids which mix together technological developments in cable television, telephone-line transmission, computer science, and satellites. This creates a regulatory nightmare for government agencies which operate under laws designed to separate the computer, telephone, and television industries. These developments may be hindered if control of the new communication systems is in the hands of the moguls at the major networks and their counterparts in existing industries such as the telephone and data-processing companies. In the standard grabbing for money and monopolistic control, such companies might want to use these developments for private ends and prevent them from reaching the public. The potential of the new communication technology does not guarantee that these companies will make exciting new services generally available. For years, people were enjoined from using any but telephone company equipment on telephone company lines. Now that the law allows the use of other equipment, we have seen a proliferation of products designed for use with telephone lines: automatic dialing, answering machines, Teletext equipment, telephone amplifiers, wireless phones that can be used anyplace in the home or office, data-servicing equipment, and many more.

However, three characteristics of the new communication systems suggest that they may indeed arrive in our homes and offices. First, they have bucked the inflationary trend of the past decade and will probably continue bucking it through the mid-1980s. Thus, while the cost of roast beef and potatoes has risen and will continue to rise, the cost of large-scale integrated circuits and memory chips (the meat and potatoes of our new technology) has declined and will continue to decline for a few more years, following the pattern established by digital watches and pocket calculators, which began as very expensive items and then plummeted in price as they became mass-produced. Digital watches that used to cost several hundred dollars are now available for eight or ten dollars. Computers costing ten or twelve thousand dollars do the work of earlier computers that cost several hundred thousand dollars. Second, the new communication systems do not require audiences in the millions to make them economically viable or socially appealing. They will find their audience through narrowcasting, rather than broadcasting, and they will serve special-interest groups. Third, most of the new communication services are two-way. People can participate in these media, not merely receive them. In the past, a relatively small group of people created the movies, television programs, and other forms of mass entertainment for the public. With the new services, many more people (in a way, everyone) will create communications for others.

Perhaps the best way to think about these new communication services is to begin with the telephone, that inexpensive, two-way, narrowcast medium which has been with us for so long. In audio, conferencing microphones and speakers can replace telephones, so ten, twenty, or more people in one room can talk freely to similar groups at other locations. A range of equipment exists which can transmit simple writing or graphics over ordinary phone lines. The "electronic blackboard" is one such device. With it, people at separate locations can talk to each other and write information which everyone can see. Another technology, called slow-scan television and facsimile transfer equipment, can send still photographs, X rays, charts, etc., over telephone lines. These systems are currently operating in some business, medical, and educational settings. A key element in their growth is the use of the telephone lines for transmission. Equipment can be plugged in wherever a phone line exists, and the cost of sending the information is the cost of a phone call.

Electronic mail also uses the telephone system. In this case, a central computer with phone lines attached acts as a postal service. A person with a modified electronic typewriter calls the central computer, then types a message for another person, who also needs a modified electronic typewriter to receive it. He or she gets the message by going to the electronic mailbox, i.e., calling the central computer. The computer then prints out the message. Electronic mail is an adaptable and growing service in business. Some expect that when the cost of a first-class letter reaches twenty-five cents, people will turn to electronic mail as an economically feasible alternative for private correspondence.

The growth of cable television is bringing about another new range of services. First, cable television has the capacity for many channels. Thus we have already witnessed the growth of several new channels of special-interest programing: all movies (Home Box Office), all sports, all news (Cable News Network). This trend will likely continue as additional narrowcast audiences are defined. Just as magazines are geared to skiers, chess players, teenage women, and other groups, cable television programing will probably pursue select non-mass audiences.

However, this is only the beginning of the changes ahead. A television cable, like a telephone line, can be used for two-way communication. The home viewer can communicate back to the program or to other viewers through the cable. The development of interactive cable television has already begun in a number of communities. The most widely known of these is the Qube two-way cable system, which was first used in Columbus, Ohio. The Qube system provides the viewer with a special box that has several buttons. These buttons communicate back to the cable studio. Viewers can answer polling questions, express their views about the program or performer they are watching, and direct how the program should proceed. The ways in which viewers "vote" can be calculated instantly and displayed on the screen for all to see. Elsewhere (Spartanburg, South Carolina), systems like Qube have been used to bring together and facilitate the work of people in educational and social services. In Rockford, Illinois, a similar system provides advanced training for teachers and firemen.

Even more exciting is a model interactive cable television system in Reading, Pennsylvania. Some twenty locations around Reading are wired as neighborhood communication centers. The interaction among the centers as the people talk to one another creates a new type of television involvement. People at home participate by calling in and speaking over a telephone connection that everyone can hear. Curiously, the interactive cable programing they create competes successfully with network programing.

A cable television channel may also be used to deliver specialized information to individual viewers. This makes use of a technology developed in Britain which allows many pages of print and graphic information to be multiplexed and combined electronically, then sent over the lines in a television signal. Using one cable television channel, it is possible to transmit eight hundred pages of print information in three seconds. Thus, a cable television channel can be used to transmit an electronic newspaper into the home, either printed on paper or projected onto a screen, or the cable channel can be connected to an electronic library and the user can go through an index and select information to be transmitted over the cable.

The problem with all of this new technology is not the equipment, which exists and works, but what to do with it now that we have it. What kinds of services, entertainment, and information do people want, and what will they buy, watch, and listen to? A few of the services and projects which have already succeeded may provide some clues about the future.

Alaska recently experimented with electronic town meetings. Via the combination of television and telephone, people were able to see the moderator and speakers, ask questions, and vote from their homes by telephone or electronic buttons. The success of the experiment may well be a sign of the future. More people watched the television town meetings than have participated in all town meetings since the founding of the state of Alaska. While voting in regular elections ran to 23 percent of the population, voting in the electronic town meetings ran to 66 percent of the population. Voters participated by voting yes or no on certain topics. Politicians who took part in the town meetings were reluctant to commit themselves early on any issue. This revealed their awareness of its political effects. Answers to research questions could be tabulated and exhibited before the next question was asked. Questionnaires could be adjusted and perfected in the course of asking the questions. Although the politicians were divided in their acceptance of this electronic concept, the program had a 90-percent share of the television audience during the broadcast.

In Philadelphia, Pennsylvania, and Phoenix, Arizona, the police departments have developed the use of two-way television to cut transportation costs and speed up the flow of communication. Some react instinctively against the use of advanced technology by a police department, but the results are impressive. In Phoenix, for example, public defenders meet with prisoner-clients over two-way picture telephones. (The prisoner-client must agree to use the system, and not all meetings are conducted over picture telephones.) This has resulted in more "meetings" between the public defenders and the prisoner-clients. At the same time, the system has reduced costs, because the public defenders can handle more clients.

In Philadelphia, witnesses to a crime can view color-slide mug shots over a two-way cable television system. The slides are centralized, but the witness can view them from any precinct house. Similarly, using this two-way cable television system, detectives can retrieve centralized information (films, fingerprints, case records) from a data bank and view it at the local precinct. In addition, video conferences and prearraignment hearings are conducted over the cable. This highly sophisticated private cable television system has significantly reduced paper and transportation costs and freed police officers to spend more time on field work.

In southern Arizona, NASA and the Indian Health Service have set up a fascinating application of advanced space technology to provide health care. A central hospital which serves the Papago Indians is linked via two-way microwave to a specially equipped truck which travels throughout the reservation (hundreds of square miles). Paramedics in the truck can conduct sophisticated tests on patients. The results are communicated telemetrically to a doctor in the central hospital. In addition, the doctor and the patient many miles away can see and hear each other. Further, the paramedic and the doctor both have instant access to computerized medical histories which are stored one hundred miles away, in northern Arizona. The NASA system is quite expensive. However, it has paved the way for other, more cost-efficient medical services between a central hospital and remote health stations or clinics. We have already seen a form of medical telemetry between individuals at home and a doctor in the hospital, via telephone lines.

In Britain, two forms of electronic print services are well under way, although neither can be classified as a success yet, because a number of gremlins need elimination. In one system, called Viewdata, a central computer contains many thousands of pages of information, from current sports results to recipes to airline schedules. Using a special decoder, a person calls the computer, and an ordinary television set displays the requested information that the computer transmits. Users can also obtain a computer printout of the information. In the other service, Broadcast Teletext, a computer at the television station contains a few hundred pages of information, e.g., television listings, movie schedules, weather, and news headlines. These pages are electronically "piggybacked" on the regular television signal. A viewer who wants to read the pages must have a special decoder that can pull them out and display them on the television screen. It is also possible to obtain a hard copy of Broadcast Teletext pages.

Viewdata, which transmits printed matter, is particularly interesting to many business interests, since it can be used for electronic shopping. Viewdata transmits information over telephone lines and is, therefore, interactive. The person in the home can not only request information, e.g., airline schedules, but also purchase services. Viewdata can be used to make an airline reservation, do catalog shopping, and reserve a table at a restaurant.

If the new communication services (or a significant portion of them) make their way into the average home and office, the social effects may be quite far-reaching. First, television network programing will lose some of its control over the mass audience. People will still watch television, but they will have access to a wider range of programs. They will also use the television set as a display screen for some information and entertainment services other than programs. They will be able to receive weather reports, traffic reports, local sports, shopping news, and the like. They can have access to any section of their newspapers and magazines, or follow the activities of local and national government. They can also use television as a ticket-purchasing service. One need neither weep over nor applaud the demise of the television networks, as they are likely to be financially involved in the new communication services which prove successful.

A significant shift in work patterns may occur. The new communication services can substitute for a portion of the business travel which now occurs. Moreover, a greater number of people will work out of their homes, using the new technology to conduct business and link them to central offices. Before locating a corporate headquarters, industries will pay greater heed to available telephone network switching, cable systems, and satellite linkups.

The potential implications of the new communication services are dramatic. Technology will mediate more and more of the communication that now takes place between individuals. This technology and the services which it does or doesn't offer will affect the quality and character of our communication with others. It may develop as the telephone did, with content determined by users. Indeed, one hopes that the new services will supplement, rather than supplant, interpersonal contact, creating new kinds of interactions among people. Developments could go either way.

The new technology could allow more sources of information to reach the public. This may break up the common information environment which television has created. In the sixties and seventies, most people received most of their information from one source: television.

The new communication technologies provide a means for instantaneous feedback from the public. Each person in his home will be able to push a button to vote or express an opinion on public issues. This may lead to more participation in politics but also to even less voting in elections than exists today. If this occurs, the logical response might be to incorporate the new communication process formally into government. People could vote directly on many laws and policy issues. In such circumstances, many elected officials might be replaced by administrators whose job would be to present issues for public voting. This might also lead to a speedup in government. Politics and laws could change more quickly. Cycles of recession and recovery might be reduced from many months to a few weeks. As information flow increases, so does social and political change.

Undoubtedly a number of problems will accompany the use of the new communication technologies in governing a country. It might be valuable to consider them in much greater depth, because technology can lead to important social and political effects which are unforeseen but inevitable. These technologies can lead to a restructuring of government. The basic reason for having a representative government is that all the people cannot themselves be at the seat of government. Therefore we call on others to be there and to speak for us. But with the new technol-

ogies, for all practical purposes we *can* be there, and we may not need representatives, because we now represent ourselves.

No one chose to give the President twenty minutes to decide the fate of the world. The design of missile technology chose it. And as we perfect our mastery of the second god, we must realize that we have given the god we created the power to change us and our ways.

Index

Tony Schwartz has made commercials for over four hundred corporations and products, designed sound for sixteen Broadway shows, produced dozens of records, and been a four-time winner at the Cannes film festival. For more than thirty years, his weekly radio program, "Around New York," was broadcast on station WNYC. As a specialist in political media, he has produced television and radio commercials for the campaigns of two Presidents, as well as for hundreds of candidates at all levels of government, from Capitol Hill to City Hall.

A professor of telecommunications at New York University, Tony Schwartz lives in Manhattan with his wife and two children.